D0443317
THIS BOOK BELONGS TO:

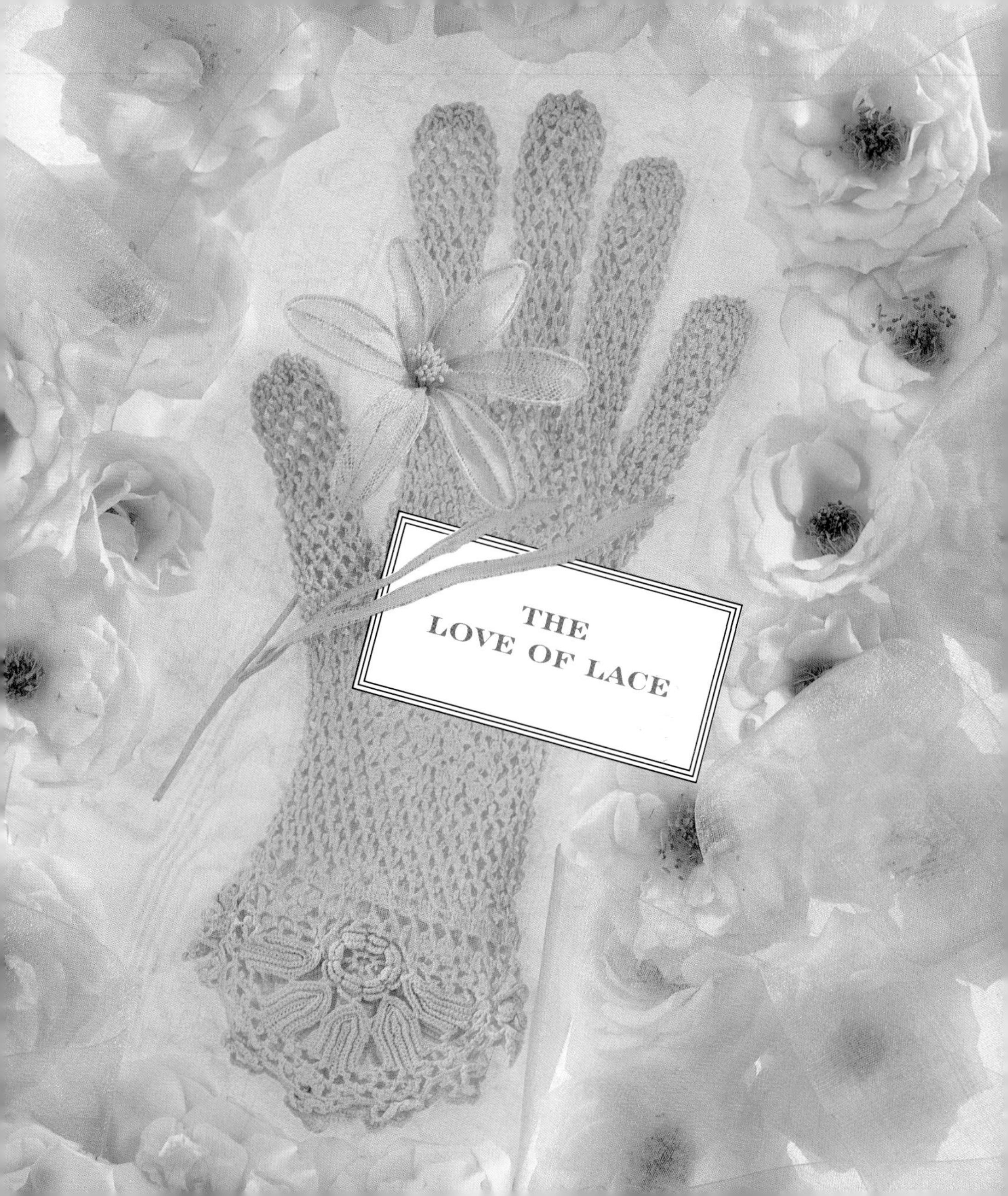
THE
LOVE OF LACE

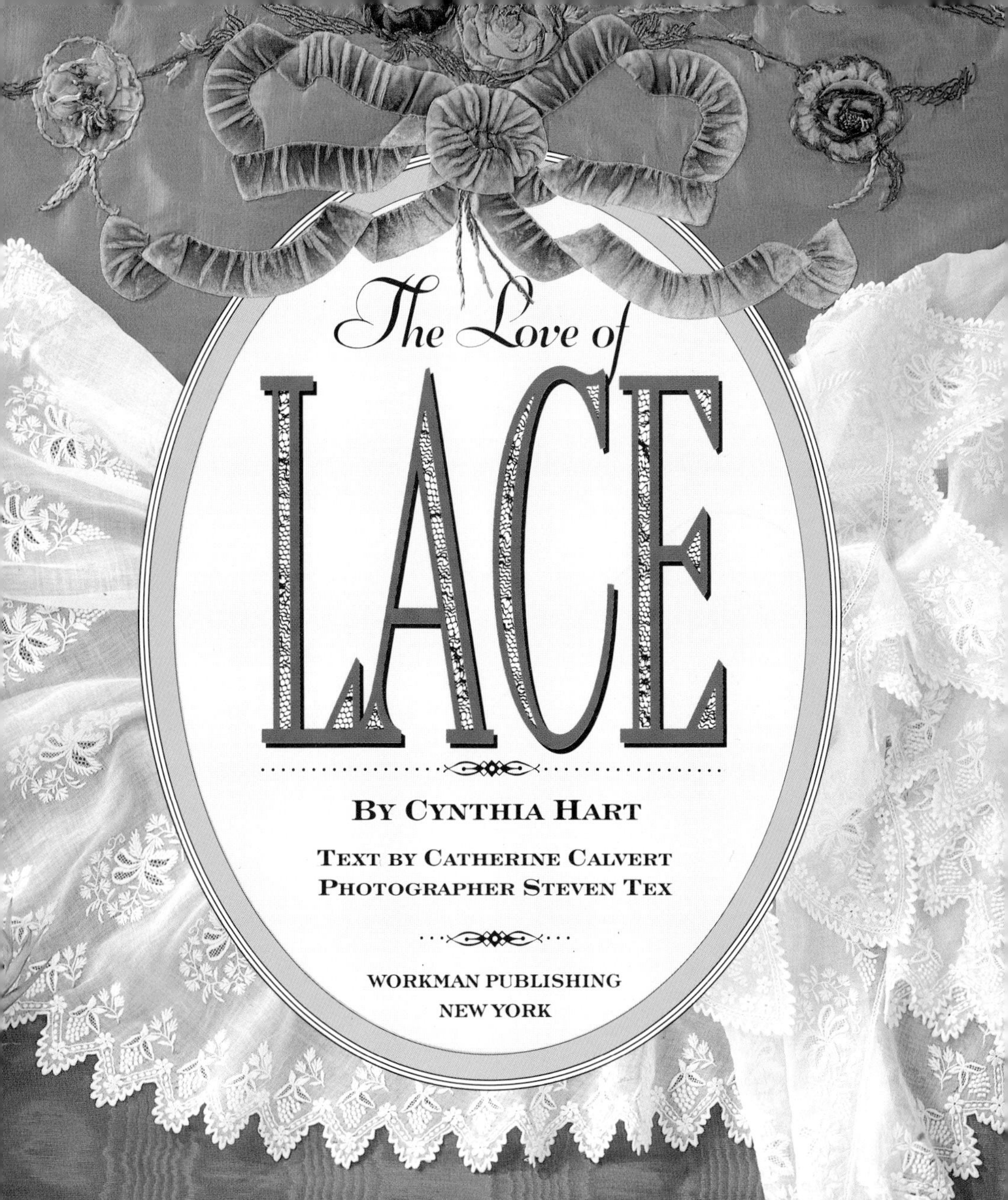

The Love of
LACE
BY CYNTHIA HART
TEXT BY CATHERINE CALVERT
PHOTOGRAPHER STEVEN TEX
WORKMAN PUBLISHING
NEW YORK

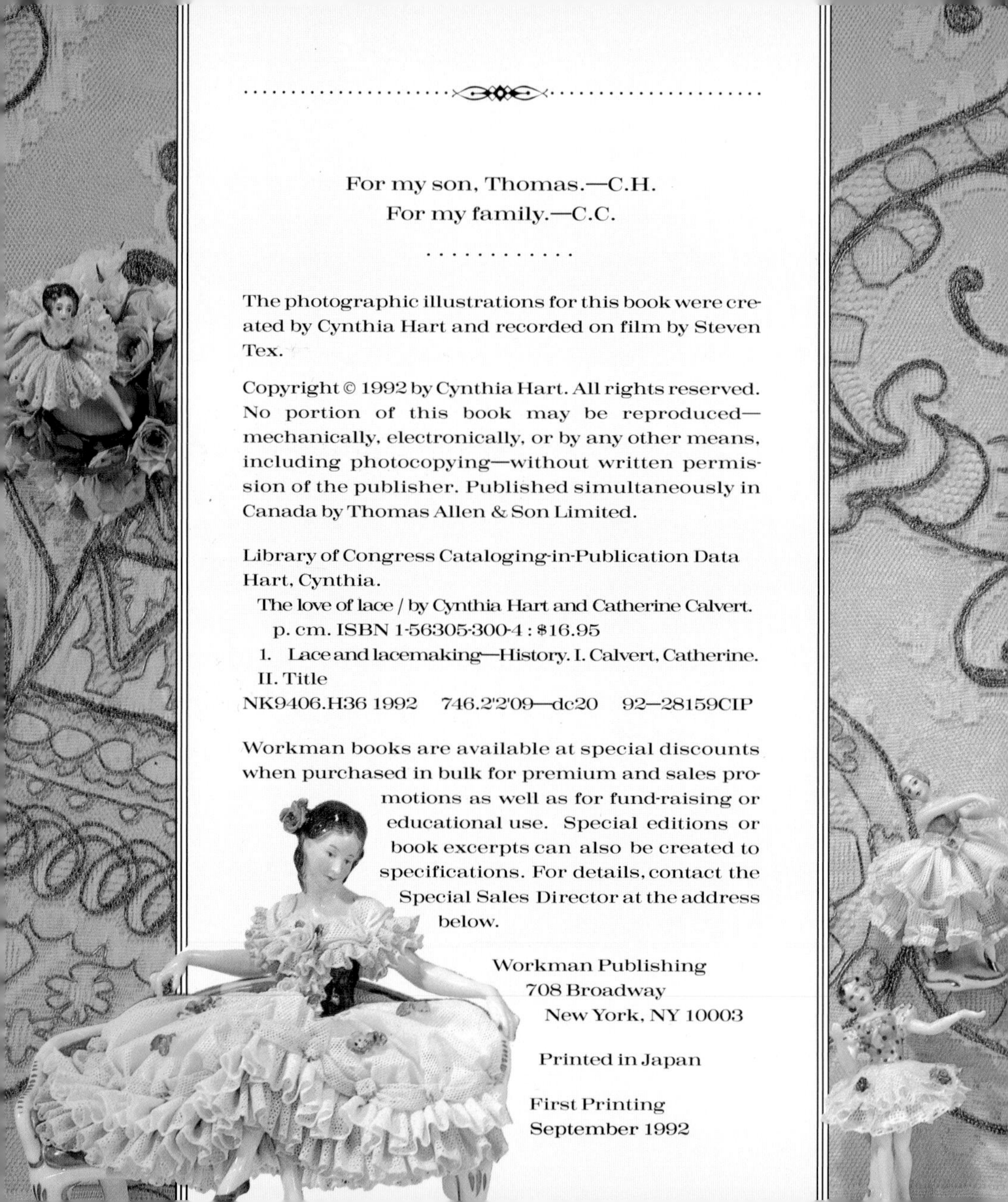

For my son, Thomas.—C.H.
For my family.—C.C.

. . . .

The photographic illustrations for this book were created by Cynthia Hart and recorded on film by Steven Tex.

 Published simultaneously in Canada by Thomas Allen & Son Limited.

Library of Congress Cataloging-in-Publication Data
Hart, Cynthia.
The love of lace / by Cynthia Hart and Catherine Calvert.
p. cm. ISBN 1-56305-300-4 : $16.95
1. Lace and lacemaking—History. I. Calvert, Catherine.
II. Title
NK9406.H36 1992   746.2'2'09—dc20   92—28159CIP

Workman Publishing
708 Broadway
New York, NY 10003

Printed in Japan

First Printing
September 1992

ACKNOWLEDGMENTS

Thank you, Kaethe and Jules Kliot, for allowing me to photograph laces and lacemaking artifacts from your private collection; for your expert advice and the use of your library; for your dedication to preserving fine laces and sustaining the art of lacemaking; for creating your store *Lacis* (making Berkeley, California, a mecca for lacelovers from around the world); and for a generosity of spirit toward my work that has helped me express my love of lace.

I would also like to give my heartfelt thanks to the following friends and associates: Jo Bidner, for her lessons and expertise; Roslyn Tunis, for moving to Oakland, California; Regina Sugrue, for the loan of laces; Virginia Makis, for sharing her love of lace; Nancy Lindemeyer, for her friendship and advice; Sally Kovalchick, Lynn Strong, and everyone at Workman Publishing, for their enthusiasm and dedication to excellence; Kathy Herlihy-Paoli, for her sensitive graphic design; Pat Upton, for her *esprit de corps;* Catherine Calvert, for her inspired "story" about lace; Mary Manning, for "Truly Lace"; Sharyn Prentiss, for her vision and lace collection; Ilene Chazanof Decorative Arts, New York City, for the loan of antique jewelry; The Dolls Corner, Scotch Plains, New Jersey, for the loan of antique dolls; Steven Tex, for his photographic expertise and sunny disposition; and Harumi Ando, for being there.

—Cynthia Hart

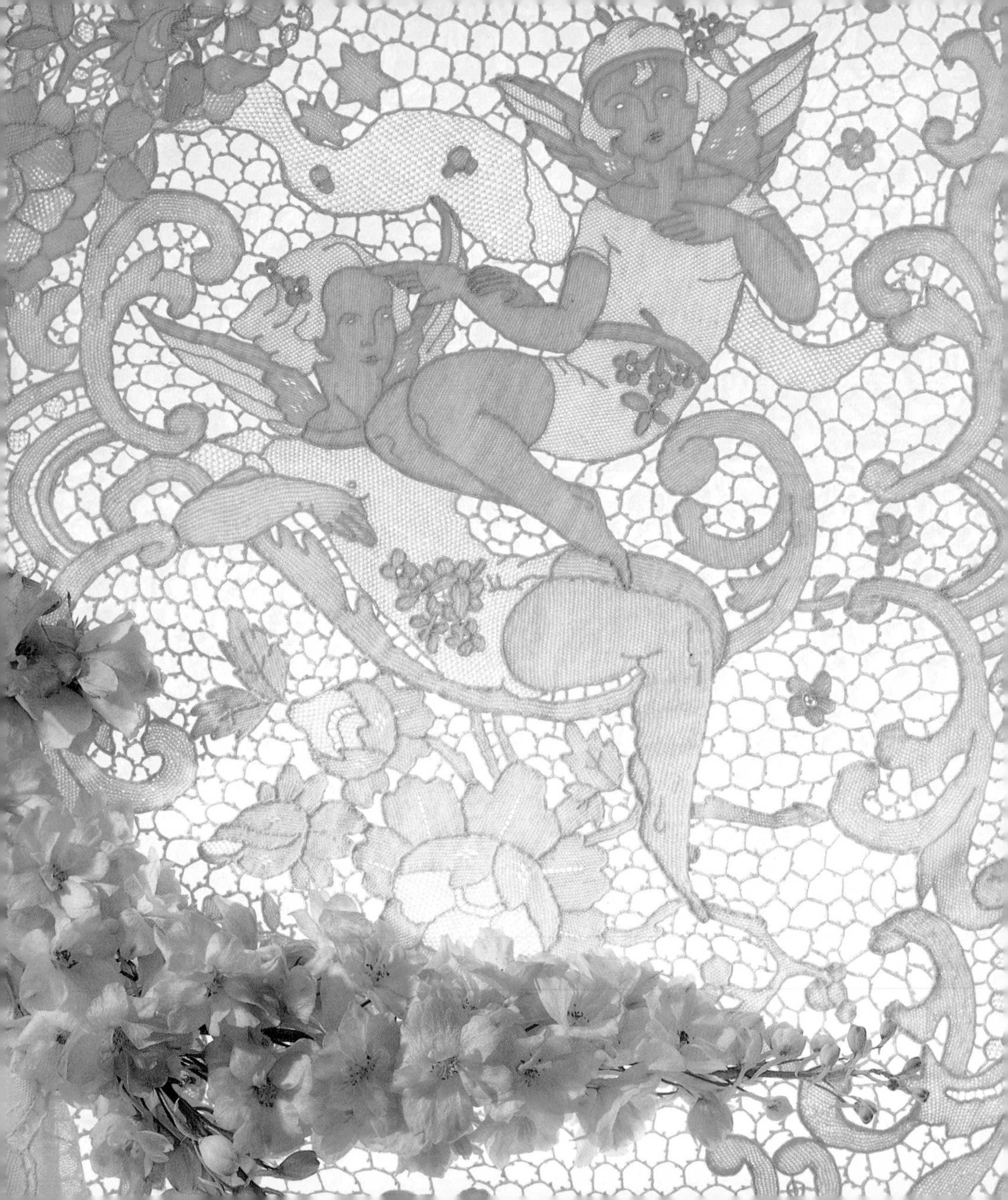

CONTENTS

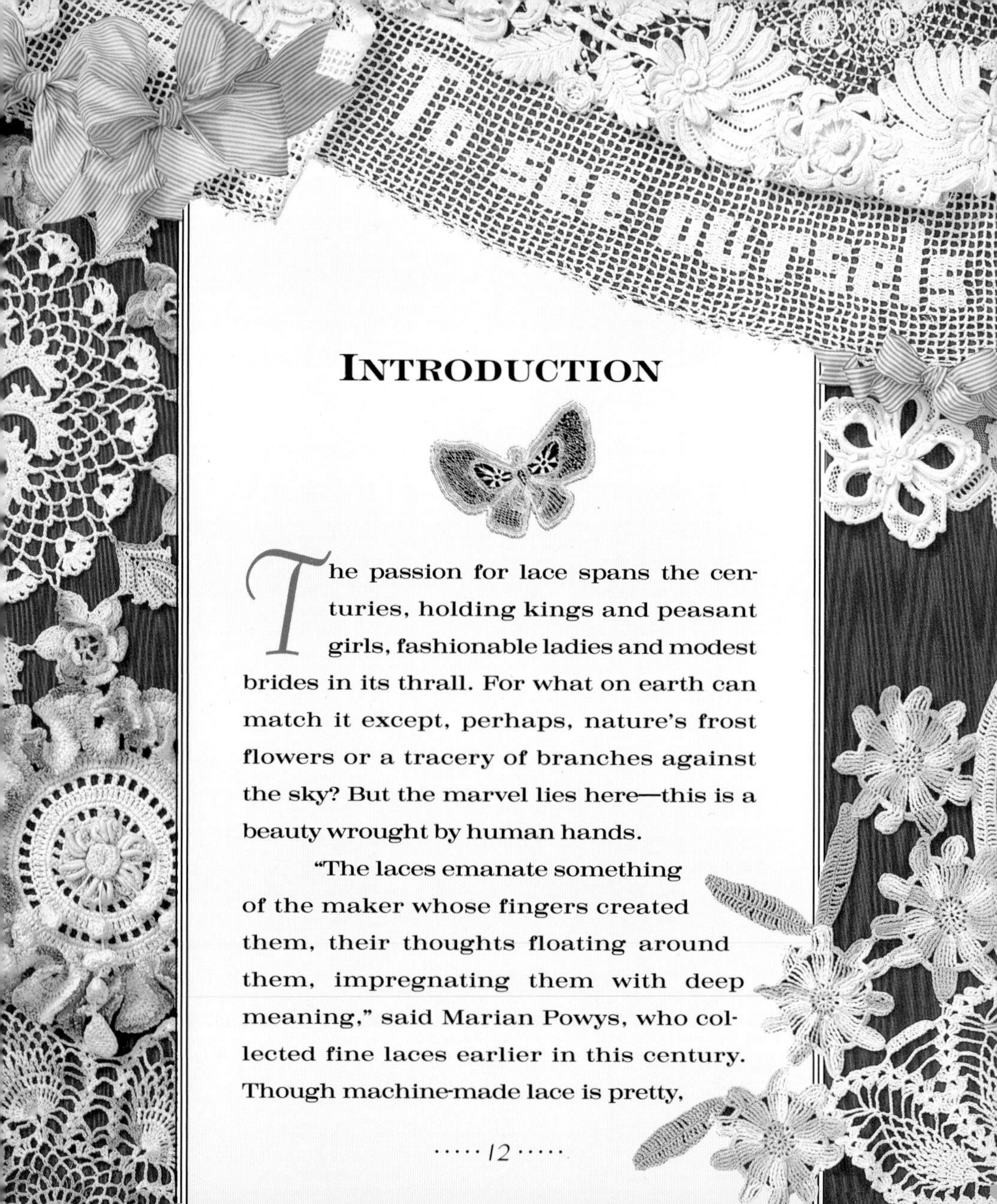

INTRODUCTION

The passion for lace spans the centuries, holding kings and peasant girls, fashionable ladies and modest brides in its thrall. For what on earth can match it except, perhaps, nature's frost flowers or a tracery of branches against the sky? But the marvel lies here—this is a beauty wrought by human hands.

"The laces emanate something of the maker whose fingers created them, their thoughts floating around them, impregnating them with deep meaning," said Marian Powys, who collected fine laces earlier in this century. Though machine-made lace is pretty,

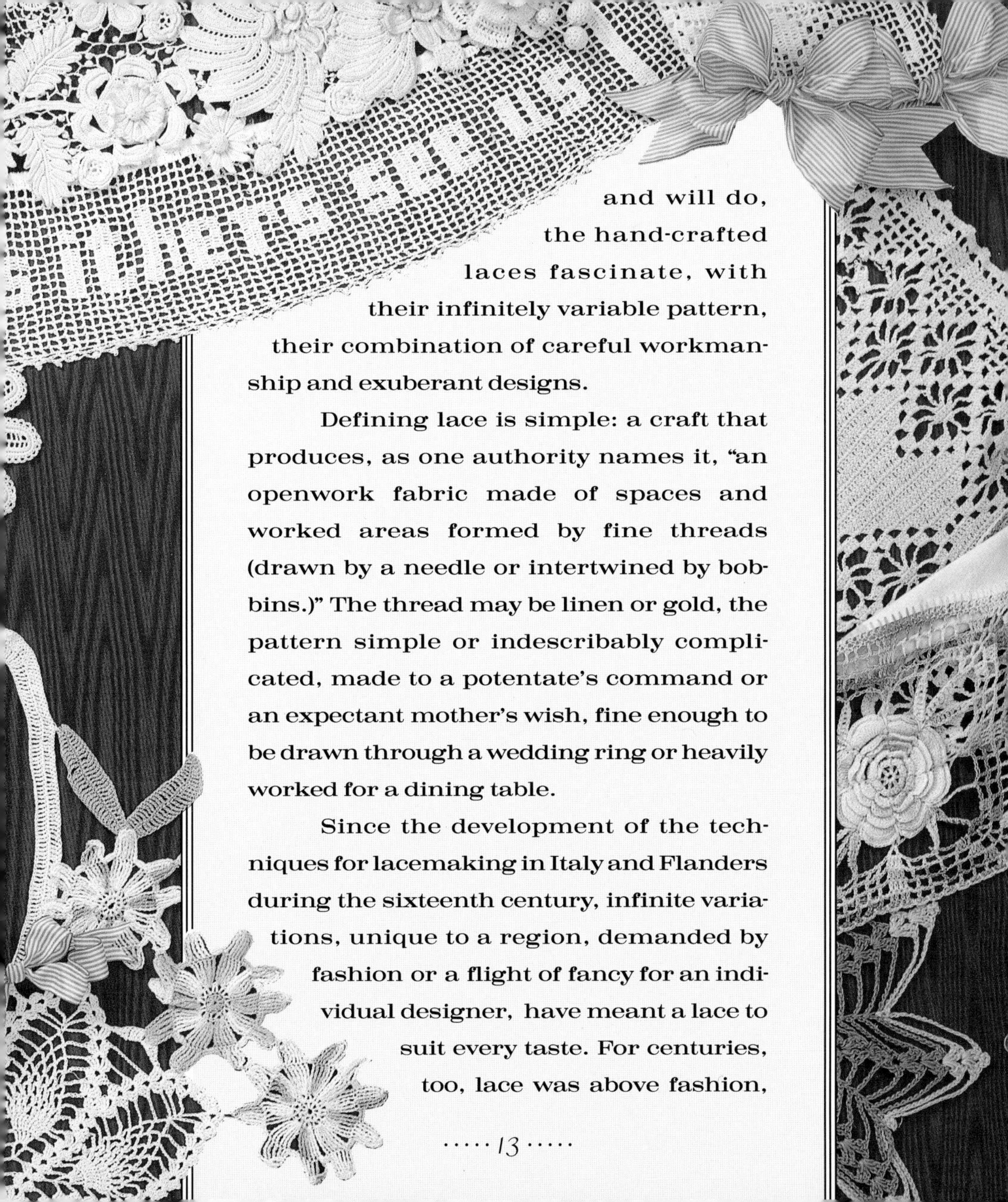

and will do, the hand-crafted laces fascinate, with their infinitely variable pattern, their combination of careful workmanship and exuberant designs.

Defining lace is simple: a craft that produces, as one authority names it, "an openwork fabric made of spaces and worked areas formed by fine threads (drawn by a needle or intertwined by bobbins.)" The thread may be linen or gold, the pattern simple or indescribably complicated, made to a potentate's command or an expectant mother's wish, fine enough to be drawn through a wedding ring or heavily worked for a dining table.

Since the development of the techniques for lacemaking in Italy and Flanders during the sixteenth century, infinite variations, unique to a region, demanded by fashion or a flight of fancy for an individual designer, have meant a lace to suit every taste. For centuries, too, lace was above fashion,

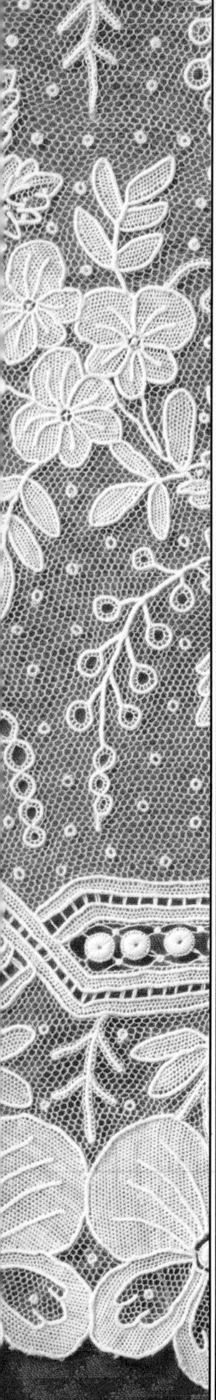

more a passion for which noblemen pledged their lands, and ladies, perhaps, their virtue. Lacemaking was a way to pass the time for the accomplished gentlewoman as well, a parlor art for pretty hands. Until well into this century, lacemaking meant some small independence for the woman whose dextrous fingers could weave taut threads of linen into beauty unsurpassed.

Today, when we approach lace, we bear the weight of memory with our appreciation. Lace is no simple trim. We touch a ruffle and think of eighteenth-century coquettes, who knew this was the fabric of flirtation. We lift a bridal veil and remember the Victorians, who thought white lace expressed the language of purity, of moral perfection. We see a mantilla and think of the Spanish women who sought sanctity with their laces, and beauty, too, a crown for womanhood. We unfold a linen napkin, passed, perhaps, from a grandmother, and heavy with drawnwork and stitchery and lace rosebuds, and become aware of the dig-

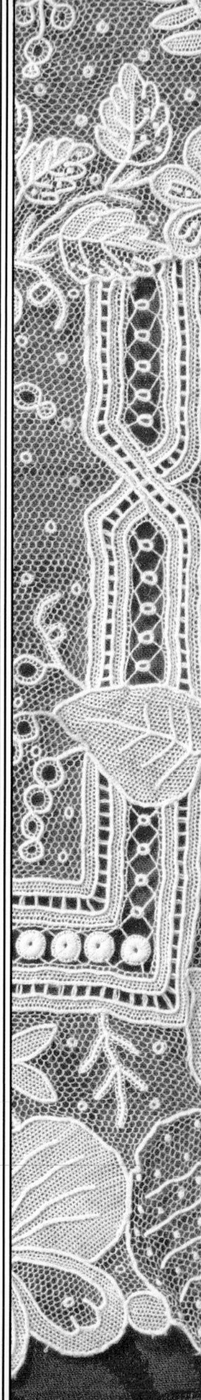

nity of such daily domestic ceremonies as dining together and those who once gathered round the table. We wander a lingerie department, where lace-frosted peignoirs enchant and a black lace bustier is sexy and amusing. Most of all, lace is a reminder of all that belongs to women, a fabric of femininity, a woman's grace, woman-wrought.

The increased recognition of lace's appeal, both for fashionable dress and as a collector's treasure, is seen in our search for ruffled Victorian dresses, romantic bed linens or stately tablecloths. Once again, we are caught in the delicate web spun by that most alluring of human creations.

Chapter One

The Legacy of Lace

"The invention of a goddess and the occupation of a queen"—these were the words of Vinciolo, the inspired designer of lace whose patron was Catherine de Médicis. And those who love lace share the tie, the delicate woven bands that link us to mighty queens, to little girls laboring by candlelight, to the goddess of inspiration who first spun magic from a bit of flaxen thread.

Needle lace, the finest flowering of the needleworker's art, was born in the simple darning that finished off an edge of fabric or mended a tear. From utility to creativity is but a short step, and soon bits of thread were teased loose and braided at the end, or a plain undergarment was treated to a wisp of embroidery in white thread. By the 1400s, cutwork began to appear as threads were cut and pushed apart,

and the opening embroidered round, for the first appearance of a lace effect. Soon ladies of the castle, for whom stitchery was a required skill as well as an amusement, and who insisted upon beautifully decorated clothes for their grander life, began to experiment with threads of silver or gold and with more fanciful bits of cutwork.

As the Renaissance began to spread through Europe, Venice stood supreme as a center for world trade, production of luxuries, and life lived among riches. Needleworkers from as far away as China came to work there, and traders brought goods from exotic lands. Venetians probably saw the decorated net-

The exquisite point plat de Venise shown here dates to the seventeenth century.

work that was an old tradition in places like Syria and Persia. (Some of the first lacelike network ever recorded came from Egyptian tombs, used to decorate shrouds.)

By the mid-sixteenth century, a new style of needlework had evolved in Venice. By drawing a design on parchment, tracing its outlines in fine thread and filling in with a wide variety of stitches, a delicate, decorative shape of stitchery could be made, then snipped from its background and used to trim a neckline, a tablecloth, a vestment. The freedom and fancy of the new needle lace, called *punto in aria* ("point in the air"), fired the imagination of designers, who no longer had to take into account the rigid geometry required by cutwork, with its crosshatch of warp and woof threads. Now the needleworkers' fingers could fly—shaping delicate rosettes, tracing figures from history or myth, spangling the material like stars at night. Seaweed, birds, vines and flowers, human figures, urns, the tree of life—all found their representation here, as if drawn in snowflakes.

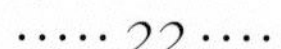

LACIS

Derived from a Latin word meaning "noose" and the source of our own word "lace," lacis is the decoration of square net by weaving fiber through the web. Crusaders returning from the East may have introduced this age-old form of embroidery, which gained popularity among the courts of Europe. The craft gained new followers in the Victorian era, when it was used most often to decorate bed and table linens.

Protected Patterns

In the early seventeenth century, master lace designer Federico Vinciolo's book of patterns was copied widely, not only by the lacemakers but by marbleworkers and bookbinders as well. Gradually, with the growth of the lace industry, regional designs flourished and pattern books fell into disuse. Each region's techniques became such closely guarded secrets that sometimes the complete patterns were withheld from the lacemakers themselves.

Ladies of accomplishment embraced the art. Little girls were set to samplers; their mothers stitched beside them, dedicating their work to the Church or to their own ornament. A new industry bloomed as the master designers and stitchers of Venice produced yard after yard for a world that now considered lace the very mark of refinement and wealth. The techniques of working the central motifs and the threads that linked them (called brides, or "legs") were taught, too, through pattern books; between 1525 and 1600, 140 such books were published, 100 of them in Venice. Constant experiment, to please a customer or a needlewoman, soon developed new motifs that became linked to a particular place or craftspeople; designs by Bartolomeo Danieli, for instance, often included curves and wreaths round a central motif of a vase of flowers. Other designs included representations of contemporary enthusiasms—"Indians," for instance, as the New World was explored, or tulips and narcissi as these

Portrait in Lace

The imposing lace ruffs and collars worn by Elizabeth I are seen in her portraits as the underpinning of her majesty and wealth. The Queen's wardrobe list enumerated hundreds of lace-trimmed garments, from petticoats trimmed in gold lace to a night coif of white cutwork touched with silver.

flowers were introduced by Dutch trade with the Indies.

Far to the north, in Flanders, another form of lace had evolved during this same period. Called bobbin lace, it was certainly known in Venice, but the master practitioners lived among the flax fields of Flanders, with easy supplies of fine, strong white thread. The *passementiers* of the Lowlands had a long history of weaving braids, either on looms or with bobbins and pins on pillows. Now this craft was translated into lacemaking, the thousands of bone or ivory bobbins holding thread that, twisted and woven by hand, formed long strips or motifs of fine lace. Prized for its delicacy, bobbin lace could also be combined with needle lace for an extraordinarily handsome effect.

In the courts and cathedrals of Europe, exquisite examples of the lacemaker's art began to adorn the apparel of the wealthy and powerful, used as trim, as overlays to printed fabrics, or, gathering full attention, as collars and cuffs. Less high-placed individuals could only covet such elegance, for lace was more precious than gold.

One lacelover's marriage helped spread lace fashions from Italy to France. Catherine de Médicis had brought her lacemakers with her when she married the future Henry II of France in 1533, as well as her own skills in the craft. When she died, she left behind several sets of elaborate lace bed hangings and caskets filled with thousands of squares of lacework, ready to be placed on a dress or a cloth.

Later French monarchs and their courts decorated themselves with veritable waterfalls of lace at throat and wrist and knee. Louis XIV's minister Henri Colbert abducted Italian and Flemish workers and underwrote lacemaking establishments in cities apart from Paris. Each developed distinctive styles that were prized by buyers

Sumptuary Laws

From the first appearance of lace, mighty princes regulated precisely who could wear it and in what amount. Rulers were concerned that everyone know his place—King Henry II of France complained in 1576 that there were at present "no distinctions between the commoners and the nobles." Controlling the type and amount of lace permitted also helped stem the flow of money to foreign lacemaking centers.

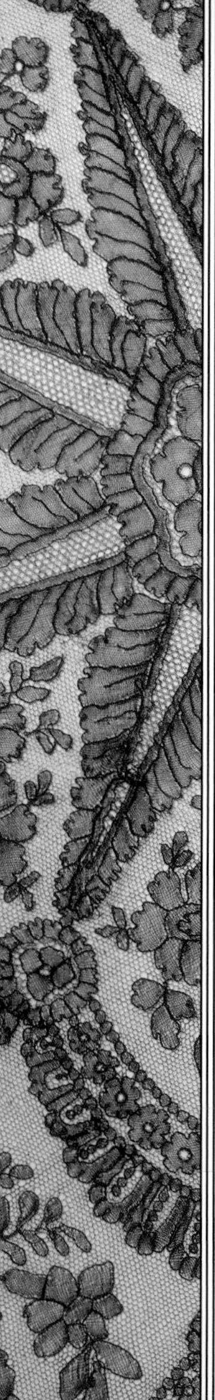

and, later, collectors, who loved the deep relief provided by the cord stiffened with horsehair in Alençon, or the firm outlines and creamy solidwork of Valenciennes.

In England, too, royal patronage set the style. Elizabeth I was known for her love of lace, her magnificent ruffs like great billows of ocean foam. Mary, Queen of Scots, whiled away the long days of her imprisonment with her needle, leaving her rich treasury of laces to the four women who had served her. France's turmoil helped England's small lace industry; when the Edict of Nantes sent the Huguenots from France, many silk- and laceworkers came to England and set up their pillows and needles in London or the provinces. English lace never quite matched that of the Continent, although Englishwomen had been making lace since before the sixteenth century. Called "bone lace," it was woven on pillows using simple bone sticks as bobbins.

Emigrating Englishwomen carried the craft to America, where it was a parlor art that might appear on a little girl's sam-

The Lace Mantilla

Spanish women have long been identified with their mantillas—the beautiful scarves of white or black lace worked in styles such as Chantilly or blonde. In the early nineteenth century, some twelve thousand women and children labored to produce mantillas for Spain and its colonies. So honored was this symbol of a woman's dignity that it could not be confiscated for debts.

pler or among a well-bred young lady's attributes. Ipswich, Massachusetts, was the only real center for American manufacturing when women who came from the Midlands in the seventeenth century brought their skills and made lace to be sold or bartered for tea or sugar, or other necessities. Though the Puritans had scorned the needless furbelows of lace, there was enough demand by less narrow minds that in 1790, for instance, 41,979 yards were made, and sold, there. Throughout the colonies, there were dandies as fond of their lace as those in Europe; even George Washington sat for his portrait in a fine cravat of French lace.

At the height of the taste for lace, almost thirty percent of the work force of Europe was engaged in some portion of its production, earning for the most part just a few pennies for their labor.

A Romance of Lace

Romantic legend has it that lace began with a rose and a woman's love. Before riding off to war, a gallant knight would present his lady with a full-blown rose. Day by day, she would watch and pine for him as the rose faded and its petals dropped. Each fallen petal would be stitched to the rose—till all dried and fell away, and the knight's lady was left with a bit of lace in her hand.

“The real good of a piece of lace, then, you will find, is that it should show, first, that the designer of it had a pretty fancy; next, that the maker of it had fine fingers; and lastly, that the wearer of it has worthiness or dignity enough to obtain what is difficult to obtain, and common sense enough not to wear it on all occasions.”

....

JOHN RUSKIN

While at times men also practiced the craft, finding it more remunerative than the plough, piecework production was primarily the province of women.

Training usually commenced at the age of five, when little girls began with a simple pattern worked with a few bobbins and suitable for an edging. Many learned their skills at convents or lace schools; others were apprenticed to lacemakers or were taught at their grandmother's knee. Most specialized in the lace of their region, but often, too, in background meshing, or flowers, or the production of linking lines. Rarely did lacemakers craft their own patterns, called "prickings." Other specialists drew the design, often taken from a pattern book. An overseer would gather all the individual pieces, then have them sewn delicately together for works of any size.

The careful labor was done under difficult conditions. Women rose with the

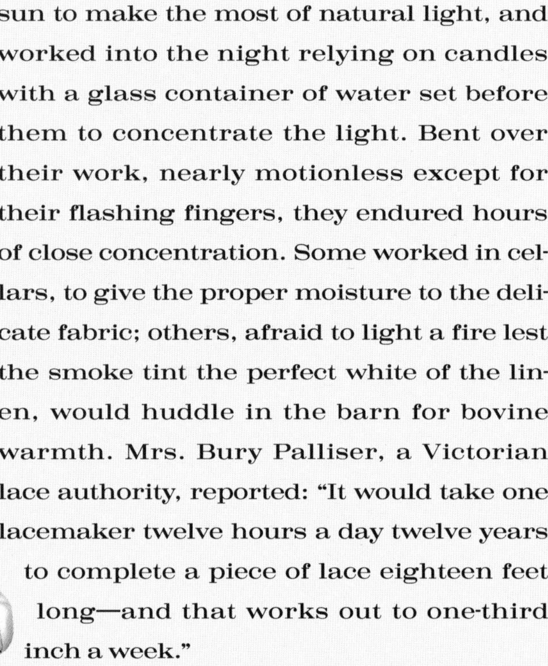

sun to make the most of natural light, and worked into the night relying on candles with a glass container of water set before them to concentrate the light. Bent over their work, nearly motionless except for their flashing fingers, they endured hours of close concentration. Some worked in cellars, to give the proper moisture to the delicate fabric; others, afraid to light a fire lest the smoke tint the perfect white of the linen, would huddle in the barn for bovine warmth. Mrs. Bury Palliser, a Victorian lace authority, reported: "It would take one lacemaker twelve hours a day twelve years to complete a piece of lace eighteen feet long—and that works out to one-third inch a week."

Conditions were perhaps better in the lace schools, where a girl had her own little bed and a clean, well-lighted place to work. But the regimen was unbending, with even the littlest girls allowed only a half-hour break twice a day and an hour at its end for school lessons. "The girls had to stick ten pins a minute, or six hundred an hour," said

Lace Look-Alikes

Though the first machine-made lace was crude, techniques rapidly improved. Now, with the designers having become quite adept at their task, machine laces have taken on the names and patterns of the earlier handmade laces. Most such laces, however, are marked by a flat finish and extreme irregularity in the stitching.

"Lace is that aspect of the poetry of dress which corresponds to the poetry of life."

MARION POWYS
EARLY TWENTIETH-CENTURY COLLECTOR OF FINE LACES

Mrs. Palliser, "and if at the end of the day they were five pins behind, they had to work for another hour."

The early years of the nineteenth century saw a new sobriety. The Revolution had rolled across France, and her citizens were in no mood for frills or peacockery. As demand disappeared, almost two-thirds of the French laceworkers lost their livelihood. Lace became the province of the lady, and of the nursery, or was reserved for lingerie.

A second revolution also changed the life of the laceworker: the industrial revolution had produced machines capable of making net, which could be embroidered for a lacelike effect. Looms that could be set to weave an infinite variety of patterns, in almost any width or length, meant that lace of all sorts was easily obtainable. By mid-century, the new lace was everywhere as the middle classes happily bought it by the yard at their local dry goods stores.

As the makers of lace put

down their needles, however, appreciation of lace as a craft was revived. International expositions, such as the one at England's Crystal Palace in 1851, displayed extraordinary lace that enticed Victorian ladies to take up lacemaking as a hobby. "Needle and Bobbin" societies taught techniques, ladies' magazines printed patterns, and the flash of a needle was seen among the tea cups in the finest of parlors. Great collectors also turned their attention to lace, and it is to their credit that some of the most precious antique laces have survived to this day. J.P. Morgan was prominent among the new lace fanciers, as were Gertrude Whiting and Alfred Lescure. An Englishwoman, Marian Powys, opened her Devonshire Lace Shop in New York, which soon became the center for those who loved the lace of history.

And so, with these delicate filaments of fancy, a new generation is tied to those who have gone before. As we hold a bit of lace in our hands, we feel in its fragile flowers, its flying arabesques, the threads that pull together 500 years of tradition.

Chapter Two

The Language of Lace

Reaching across time, lace fashions speak of high places and base passion, of purity, and promises made. The sweet simplicity of designs in white thread, like a flurry of snowflakes, the potent mysteries of black lace, have never failed to weave their magic.

Three centuries ago, lace spoke of power, both spiritual and temporal. The Church commandeered the most elaborate designs for its own use, clothing its clergy in ceremonial wear whose delicate tracery revealed the beauty of God's creations in nature, as well as Crucifixion scenes and other examples of Christian iconography. Priests literally shone in the darkness of candlelit cathedrals, their gleaming white lace cloaks symbolizing both the purity and riches of the Church. Nuns would labor over their needles, making gold or silver lace to

trim a garment, weaving sacrifice and glory with each thread. Point de Venise was especially prized, for its fine linen threads and closely worked surface ensured a garment that would incite awe in the congregation. Their gaze drawn close, worshipers could pick out the wings of an angel, for instance, or the tracing of a pomegranate that symbolized eternal life.

Those who ruled more directly, the princes and dukes and queens of countries large and small, also felt the appeal of lace and set a fashion that lasted more than two hundred years. Its first flowering came in Italy, where rich traders and richer princes ornamented themselves lavishly to declare their success to the world. The new laces—expensive, rare, infinitely variable and thus unique to an owner—became a necessity. At first it was enough to edge a

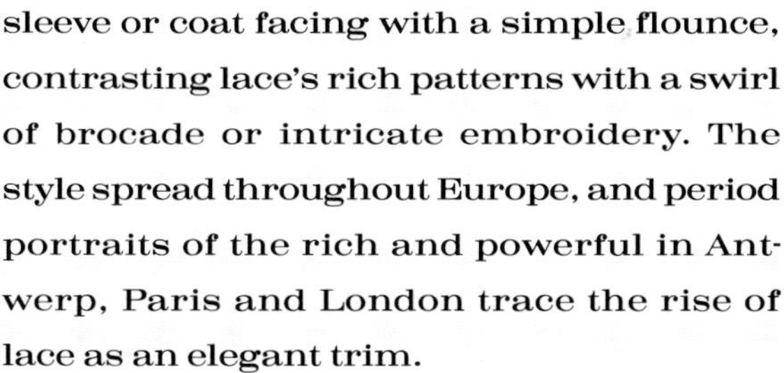

sleeve or coat facing with a simple flounce, contrasting lace's rich patterns with a swirl of brocade or intricate embroidery. The style spread throughout Europe, and period portraits of the rich and powerful in Antwerp, Paris and London trace the rise of lace as an elegant trim.

A new fashion was launched when Henry II of France ordered a large lace ruff to cover his scarred neck and courtiers set their own lacemakers to work in imitation. By 1579, gentlemen at the French court wore ruffs so large that they were hard-put to maneuver around them at dinner time; indeed, each ruff required a full twelve yards or more of material. Men and women of high degree in the capitals of Europe found the ruff flattering as well as fashionable, for it allowed full display of a lace collection in all its gossamer glory. Supported by a metal stand or starched stiff, the collars set off the face, seeming to offer it up on a platter. The English were only slightly more restrained than the French, believing the high collar set off a bejeweled earlobe

beautifully. In Venice, where the lace industry was in its glory, women favored a more modest collar that stood up tall behind them and displayed the lace more simply. French women, too, preferred a more understated collar, though it dripped in elaborate points of needle or bobbin lace.

The Calvinist Lowlands burghers, rich but solemn, found lace just as appealing, though they chose to counterpoint their dark, sober clothing with sparkling white collars and cuffs, immaculate as all else in their well-kempt countries. The collars became known as Van Dyck collars, after the Flemish artist who painted so many portraits highlighted by these broad lace expanses.

If the Renaissance made use of lace to underline power and wealth, the flirts and fops of the eighteenth century knew the power of lace to ensnare. Women's fashions called for stiff brocades and embroidered silks trimmed in great froths of lace from throat to hem, especially in the garments required for the pretty social gavotte of

"Of many Arts, one surpasses all. For the maiden seated at her work flashes the smooth balls and thousand threads into the circle, . . . and from this, her amusement, makes as much profit as a man earns by the sweat of his brow, and no maiden ever complains, at even, of the length of the day."

....

JACOB VAN EYCK

court life. Increasing expertise among the craftswomen of different lacemaking centers brought popularity to lace that was finely detailed and more fluid, gossamer fine. Soft Valenciennes lace could flutter round a sleeve; bobbin lace might outline a neckline, from which the powdered shoulders rose as if from a sea-billow. Madame de Pompadour often sat for her portrait with six broad, fluttering *engageants* at her elbows, half revealing, half concealing, her skirt sewn with tier upon tier of lacy confection. A young lady's pretty head drew attention with her lappets, the long, broad bands of lace that fluttered from a topknot, and older women knew nothing set off their snowy locks like a cap of lace. In time, the love of lace would shift down to the middle classes, and even village girls far from court life would treasure their bit of lace for Sunday best.

Eighteenth-century men also knew the enchantment of lace. Proud of their own sets of laces, they used them as cravats, to adorn their sleeves or knotted at the knee. The wardrobe of Cinq-Mars, a favorite of Louis XIV, boasted 300 lace-trimmed boots. As the century progressed, however, men began to separate themselves from things that could be considered feminine. If women loved the soft caress of bobbin lace, men preferred the stiffer, formally patterned needle lace and relegated its use to a simple frill at the wrist and a flowing cravat.

Lace had its place, but its use was increasingly circumscribed. By century's end, after bloody political revolutions and subtler revolutions in taste and sentiment, both men and women had turned away from the luxury of lace in favor of soft materials in understated designs. In France, lace had been burned and otherwise destroyed as a symbol of the despised aristocracy and virtually disappeared by the end of the Revolution. It was Napoleon II's empress Marie-Louise who loved lace for its own sake and donned it for patriotic reasons too, in hopes of reviving demand and, with it, an industry.

Fine Points

The Victorians revived the romance of the Van Dyck collar, contrasting its color and texture against rich velvets for both boys and girls.

Nineteenth-century ladies added new inflections to our understanding of lace. Now woman reigned supreme as the embodiment of goodness, of high moral standards. And lace, increasingly available as machines shuttled out their yardage, underlined her purity. Her lingerie was trimmed with lace—simple eyelet for the cottons of every day, elaborate pieces for a trousseau or the rich woman's boudoir. Lace dresses were commissioned to order, to echo corseted curves. A young lady might flirt with a lace fan, drop her lace

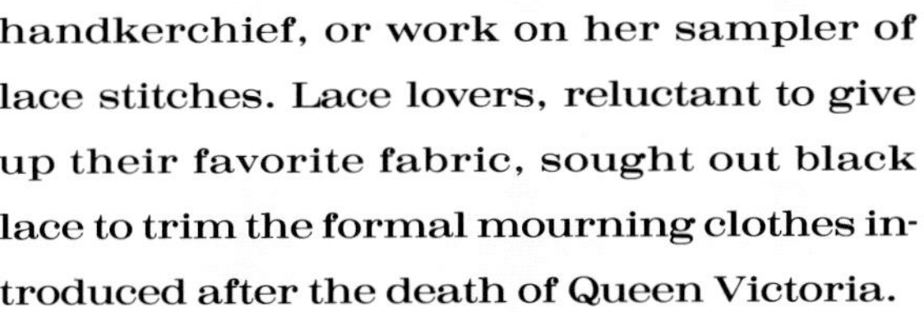

handkerchief, or work on her sampler of lace stitches. Lace lovers, reluctant to give up their favorite fabric, sought out black lace to trim the formal mourning clothes introduced after the death of Queen Victoria.

Wedding dresses, by no means always white before about 1830, also reflected the use of lace as a symbol of purity. Victoria married Albert in a dress of Honiton lace, woven with motifs of English rose and Scottish thistle. Increasingly, brides chose to appear in a cloud of white, the veil a simple square of lace caught up to flow about the face. Soon white veils of lace were a necessity for brides great and

Bridal Laces

The nineteenth-century bride who wished to look her finest on her wedding day chose precious laces for adornment. A full set of bridal laces would include not only her veil but also deep flounces of lace for her skirt, with more lace edging her petticoat; lace mitts, and perhaps a lace fan, completed the ensemble. Looked upon as a sort of dowry, such laces could be removed and used on her finest dresses as long as she lived.

A Lace Layette

Ancestral treasures surfaced with each newborn child—a christening robe of finely embroidered and artfully made white lace and lawn, or a few simple baby clothes that had been folded away in blue tissue by a sentimental mother. Everyday clothes were often finished with bobbin lace, or crochet, while the finest of needle laces were reserved for special occasions.

humble—the lace full of crests and entwined blossoms for the grander brides, while village girls were happy with a bit of reembroidered net. By century's end, a girl of distinguished parentage was glad to use her grandmother's veil, or her great-grandmother's, folded away as a family treasure a generation ago.

The vogue for lace waxed and waned, perhaps as women reinterpreted their own place in the world. The twentieth century found women of fashion searching for snippets of old lace that might be worked into skirt lengths or pretty jackets; others dyed new lace in tea or onion skins for that time-honored look. Fashion designers' tastes had more impact, and many a season they trimmed dresses with lace and made it once again fashionable. "I consider lace to be one of the prettiest imitations ever made of the fantasy of nature," said Coco Chanel, the French de-

HARPER'S BAZAR
NEW YORK, SATURDAY, JULY 15, 1893.
PUBLISHED WEEKLY.
TEN CENTS A COPY. WITH SUPPLEMENTS.
JANUARY 25, 1873.
Pin or Emery Cushion with Point Russe Embroidery.
NIGHT-VIOLET.—A NEW COLOR.
HARPER'S BAZAR.
NEW YORK, SATURD

signer. "I do not think any invention of the human spirit could have a more graceful or precise origin." She drew on lace throughout her long career, especially the dramatic and sensuous black Chantilly.

In the Twenties and Thirties, lace (machine-made or no) was adaptable to the beautifully draped simple silhouettes, whether filling in a neckline or cut for a dress. A reporter wrote in 1929 that "one sees lace everywhere. . . . Worth has the idea of slipping under the skirts of his tulle gowns a flounce of lace which lightly veils the legs without hiding them completely, and this is infinitely pretty." A woman could play at revelation yet not part with her modesty. Lace gowns could be grand and glorious, too, filled with the timeless association of wealth and privilege. After World War II, when the New Look brought a return of the lavish evening gown, Dior, Balenciaga and other designers made much use of the material, loving its grand luxe, its inescapable richness. And today, every season or two, a designer rediscovers its possibilities, mating lace to leather or sending great cascades of red lace down the runway.

Yet modern woman's most favored place for lace may be something she keeps strictly to herself. Lingerie is still lace's most popular showcase, whether used for a snippet of a brassiere, to edge a silk panty, or as a sweet scallop to a garter belt. In this private passion, women express their most personal understanding of lace and its uses. This century has given us imagery—Mae West in her black lace corset, a silk charmeuse Twenties teddy with a bit of lace at the bodice—and we make our choice, from the sweet simplicity of white to the undeniable thrill of black. All attest to the age-old power of lace—and its web of enchantment.

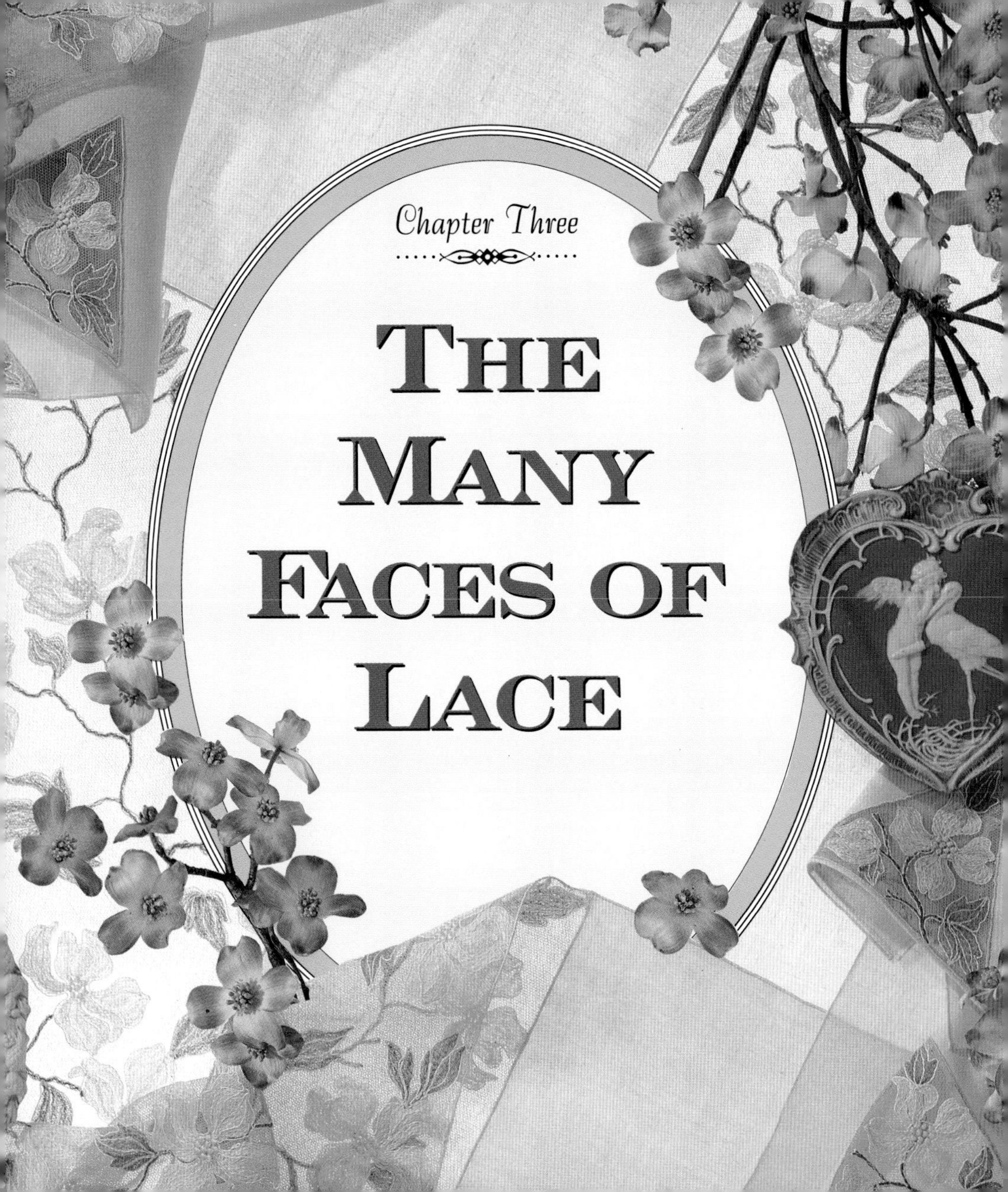

Chapter Three

The Many Faces of Lace

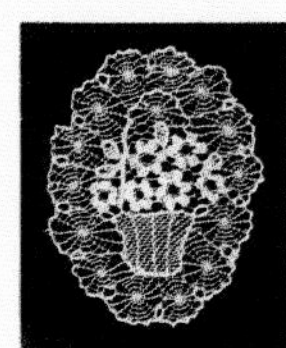

So precious was lace that a piece might be used to trim a dress, then scissored off and applied to a table linen or scarf for the space of a season, when fashions changed. Thus, through the ages, lace has added a precious finishing touch to decorative materials.

For us, a lace trimming is the very fabric of feminine allure, its use in the bedroom undeniably one of the womanly arts. Think of a bed piled high with crisp linens, their sharp edges softened by flounces of lace, with dozens of pillows of different shapes and sizes outlined by dripping laces. All are frilled, yet still inviting, each lace awaiting a touch, a caress.

Lace of this sort speaks to us of private moments, yet lace originally was a public announcement—an underlining of wealth and privilege that extended even to

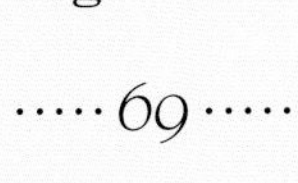

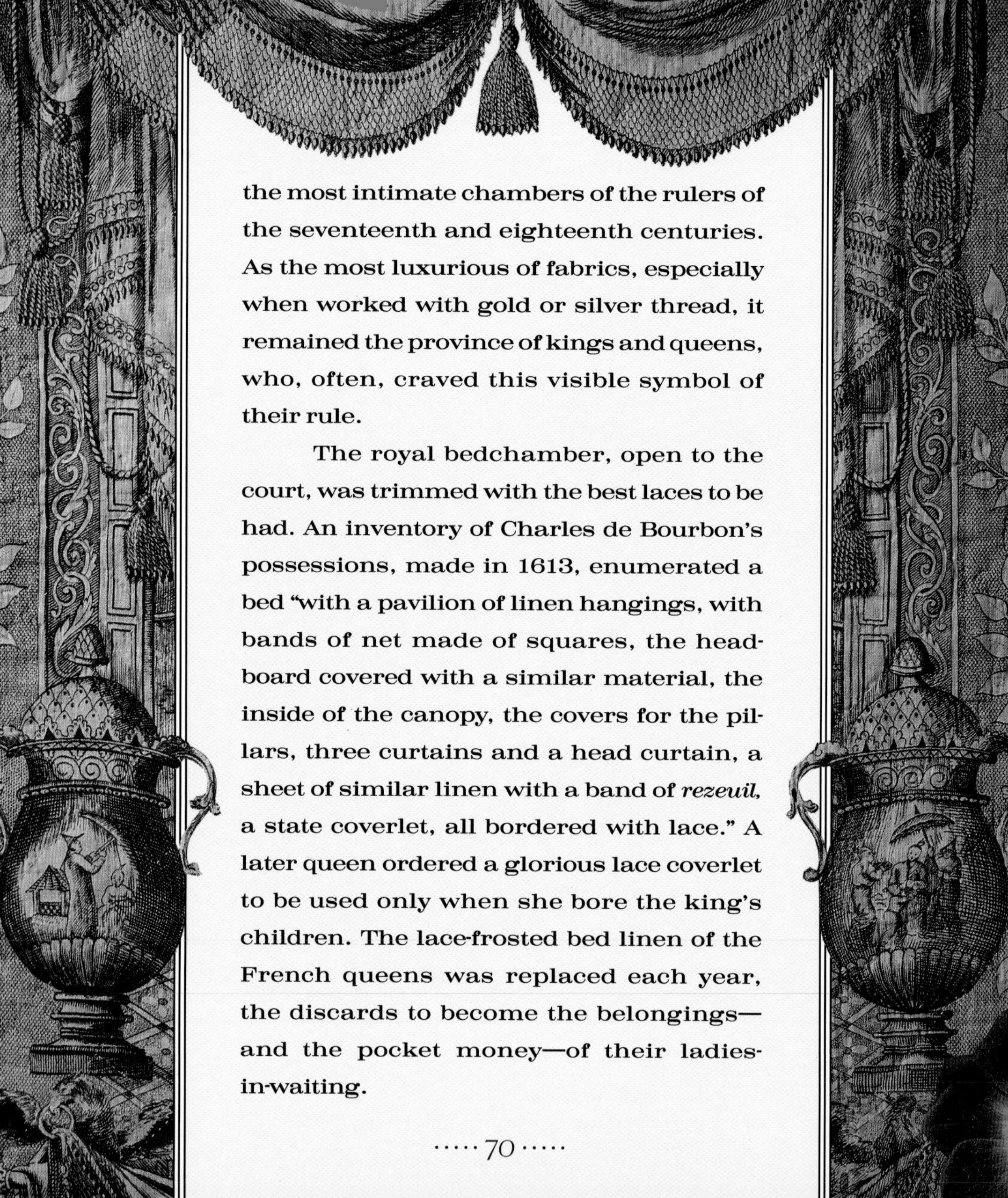

the most intimate chambers of the rulers of the seventeenth and eighteenth centuries. As the most luxurious of fabrics, especially when worked with gold or silver thread, it remained the province of kings and queens, who, often, craved this visible symbol of their rule.

The royal bedchamber, open to the court, was trimmed with the best laces to be had. An inventory of Charles de Bourbon's possessions, made in 1613, enumerated a bed "with a pavilion of linen hangings, with bands of net made of squares, the headboard covered with a similar material, the inside of the canopy, the covers for the pillars, three curtains and a head curtain, a sheet of similar linen with a band of *rezeuil,* a state coverlet, all bordered with lace." A later queen ordered a glorious lace coverlet to be used only when she bore the king's children. The lace-frosted bed linen of the French queens was replaced each year, the discards to become the belongings—and the pocket money—of their ladies-in-waiting.

A Tie to Travel

Lace was a favorite souvenir for Victorians, especially those who visited lacemaking centers such as Venice and Bruges. Wealthy young ladies who traveled to Paris for their bridal creations might also pick out a wardrobe of household linens, heavy with fine laces. Today, Ireland and Belgium are places to search for the best in handmade lace.

In England, in 1763, Queen Charlotte watched the baptism of her son the Duke of York from a bed trimmed with £3,783 worth of lace. Society leaders of the eighteenth century invited their most intimate friends to the morning receptions called *ruelles*, during which the hostess would lie abed and entertain both her gentleman callers and their ladies. Talk would swirl for hours amid lace valances as she reclined against her lace pillowcases, nestled in her lace coverlets and counterpanes.

The Victorians, too, delighted in using as much lace as a fabric could bear for their bed linen. Simple cutwork or drawnwork could suffice for every day and was a pleasant home craft for young ladies; a bureau scarf or a square or two for the dressing table was a daily pleasure. A bride-to-be was likely to commission the most romantic of pieces—bed coverlets worked with love birds, pillowcases frothy with lace. Marian Powys, writing about the early twentieth century, observed: "Ladies who are addicted to break-

DRAWNWORK

As early as the twelfth century, needleworkers learned to draw out a few threads from a bit of cloth, then embroider and decorate the remaining threads to create fanciful patterns. This drawnwork, also known as Hamburg point, Dresden point or Indian work, was especially popular among Victorian women, who found it especially useful for decorating fancy towels and table linens.

fast in bed sometimes like a little light lace on silk as a blanket cover, with an elegant bed jacket to go with it, and certainly there should be a fine lace traycloth." With care, such pieces became cherished heirlooms, casting their spell of romance to the present day.

Luncheons and formal dinners required a table covered by a length of heavily worked lace with, perhaps, linen napkins, lace-trimmed, at every place. No trousseau was complete without its lace tablecloth, as important as the bridal veil itself, to be brought out on all ceremonial occasions or left to cover the table between meals.

Separate dining rooms were rare in most homes until well into the eighteenth century, and fine tablecloths and napkins awaited the evolution of fine table manners. (Who needed a napkin when a sleeve would suffice?) Still, tablecloths were common, especially in the homes of the rich and at kings' courts; the removal of the tablecloth and the presentation of nuts, fruits and wines signaled the end of a meal. Ornamenting the table linens with embroidery and laces became the task of young girls filling their hope chests into much of this century; Belgian convent schools as late as the 1960s still drilled their girls in fine needlework, so each could leave to be married with a hope chest containing more than a dozen tablecloths, individually designed and full of lace and stitchery. Wealthy girls, too, would spend their engagement periods shopping for table linens and other household appointments, perhaps commanding some to be woven with their new initials or family crest.

Mrs. Powys prescribed the bare minimum of lacy table linen for the social bride in 1950: "Anyone who likes a good table, well-appointed, should have one large tablecloth of lace in the grand manner with matching dinner napkins, and possibly fingerbowl doilies of the same lace. . . . For

Lacy Accents

In the late nineteenth century, doilies provided a showcase for one's ability with the needle. Prettily appointing nearly every surface in the household, these bits of decorative lace were seen lining the tea tray, scattered down the dining table's expanse, cushioning each item in the china closet. Antimacassars, also known as "tidies," served to protect upholstery, especially from the hair oil called "macassar."

luncheon, a lace set made up of a scarf with oblong place mats and napkins to match. . . . A finer lace scarf can be used on the table between the meals with a lovely vase of flowers. On occasional tables, a small piece of lace is charming and practical for keeping the well-polished table from being stained by dampness at the bottom of . . . the cocktail glass or the teacup. A lace tea tablecloth can be made of very fine lace about forty-five inches square or more, and round for a round table with small matching napkins and possibly lace for the tray."

The kind of lace chosen has always been a matter of personal taste, though the heavily worked, richly designed Milanese or Flemish laces were reserved for very formal occasions when, in the Victorian tradition, the table was laden with several kinds of glasses, battalions of silver cutlery and ornate centerpieces. Others might choose the very delicate but elaborate working of point de Venise, or a fanciful bit of Irish crochet. A tea cloth, with its smaller

> “And here the needle plies its busy task,
> The pattern grows, the well-depicted flower,
> Wrought patiently into the snowy lawn,
> Unfolds its bosom, buds and leaves and sprigs,
> And curling tendrils, gracefully dispersed,
> Follow the nimble fingers of the fair—
> A wreath that cannot fade of flowers that blow
> With most success when all besides decay.”

....

WILLIAM COWPER

scale, and its use as the focal point of a gathering of observant and talkative ladies, might be a triumph of stitchery; some exist that are like samplers, a dictionary of all a stitcher's mastery of the art. More important, gathering a fine stock of linen and seeing to its care and preservation was the homemaker's crowning task, with lace its chief ornament.

Perhaps the most obvious use of lace in the home came at the window. Lace curtains are an old tradition, their pretty designs providing privacy and softening the light. Starched and snowy-white, they were a housewife's pride.

As glass became more common, and window openings enlarged, householders needed something other than simple shutters or colored glass to block a window—something that would let in air while veiling a room's interior. The

lace that was loved for ornament was soon adopted as trim for lengths of white muslin or other fabrics used to drape windows. The richer the household, the more lavishly trimmed the curtain—an effective way to announce the wealth of those who lived within. Too, everyone loved the graceful light the lace curtain afforded, the sun sketching shadows of roses and meshwork across the floor as the day progressed.

It was the development of machine-made panels early in the nineteenth century that set off the fashion of hanging panels of lace at the window in tall-ceilinged great houses as well as country cottages. The Victorian passion for pattern on pattern was well served when elaborately worked curtains and roller blinds could be hung as part of an assemblage of swags and rosettes and draperies. The decorating pages of magazines advertised such items as a "Machine-Made Panel Lace designed in the 'Oriental' style, to go with Lacquered Furniture and other house furnishings reflecting the arts of Asia"—this for a panel of

lace emblazoned with chrysanthemums and flying cranes. Such work would serve a sophisticated city parlor; the country house windows would be hung with chintz draperies, and an inner lace panel of more naturalistic wildflowers and bluebirds.

By early in the twentieth century, tastes had changed and less elaborate designs were desired. The greater use of plate glass meant wider expanses, unfettered by crossbars, that enabled decorators to choose machine-made lace curtains with delicate all-over designs. Such patterns were copied from historical designs derived from the 500-year history of lace, or simple sprays of flowers and foliage calculated to produce, as one writer in 1919 stipulated, "lace curtains, suited to every pocketbook, in an almost infinite variety of radiant gauze-like fabrics."

Today, traditional lace curtains continue to please the eye, whether viewed inside or out, as they temper the light with their delicate designs.

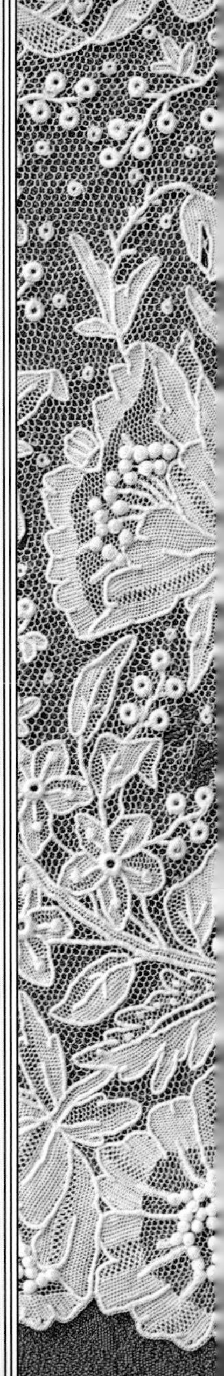

Chapter Four

THE FINE ART OF LACE

BATTENBERG LACE

Created in the 1890s, Battenberg lace was wildly popular as a woman's handicraft. Hours of careful stitchery around braids of silk or linen, selected for their beauty and durability, would result in a luxurious collar, doily or tablecloth. Newly made Battenberg from China, now commonplace, is likely to be of cotton.

There is something so essentially personal about antique lace, a bit of preciousness that one knows was treasured once and will be again. Some of us are drawn to the history woven into each individual piece and to those who loved it in the past: where is the bride who wore this veil, the happy wife who topped her sheets with a snowy edging? Others develop a passion for the stitchery itself, absorbed by the intricacy of a pattern, the matchless measure of its maker.

From admiring to collecting is a short passage, and we are in the midst of another revival of interest in owning lace. What once could be carried off for a few dollars from a dusty pile of linens in an antique shop now commands much, much more, as women raised on wash-

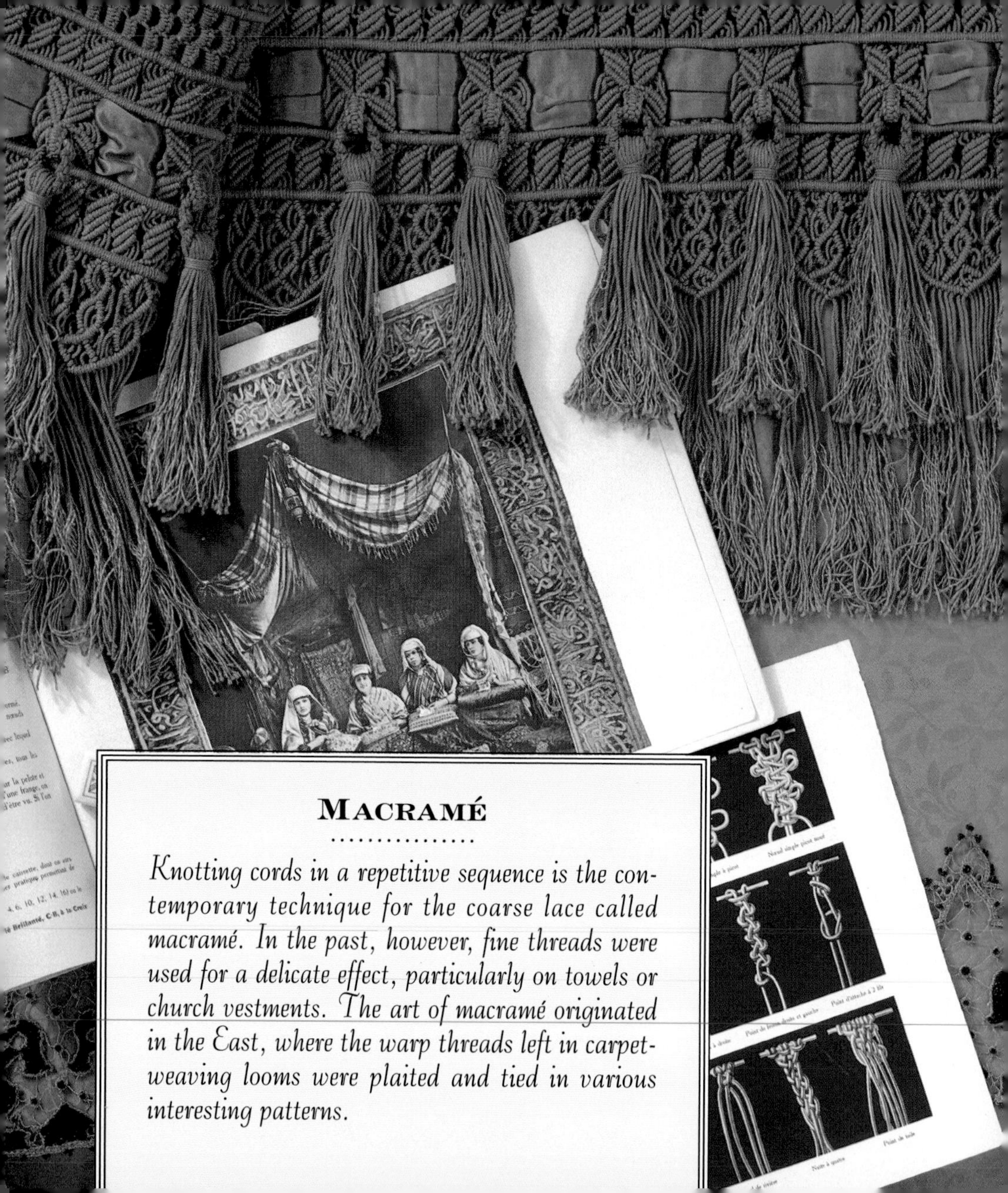

MACRAMÉ

Knotting cords in a repetitive sequence is the contemporary technique for the coarse lace called macramé. In the past, however, fine threads were used for a delicate effect, particularly on towels or church vestments. The art of macramé originated in the East, where the warp threads left in carpet-weaving looms were plaited and tied in various interesting patterns.

and-wear cultivate their new interest in linens and lace, for the home and for fashion. The lucky ones can use the well-loved, well-preserved tablecloths and pillowslips of their grandmothers and great-grandmothers, perhaps folded away when the fashions changed a generation ago. Others enjoy the hunt, at tag sales and shops, or visit the dealer who specializes in antique lace and lace-trimmed articles. A very few try the craft themselves, relearning the timeless patterns of traditional laces, and work on their own pillows and patterns. Some contemporary craftspeople have discovered that lace techniques can be used for works of art that bear no resemblance to what has been produced in the last 300 years of lacemaking.

Craftsperson or collector, learning more about the techniques that were taught in lace schools and gentlewomen's parlors, at convents and farmhouse fire-

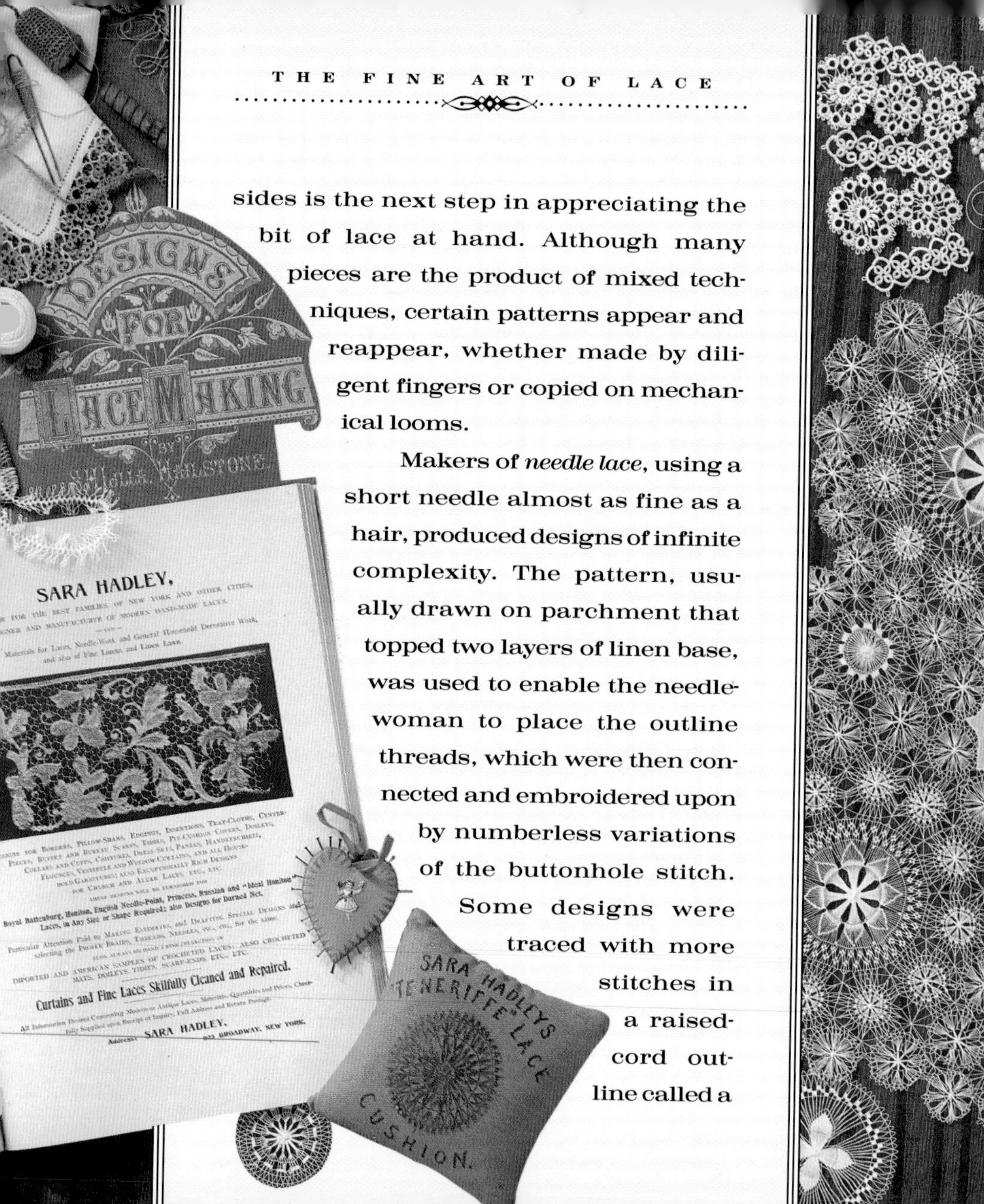

sides is the next step in appreciating the bit of lace at hand. Although many pieces are the product of mixed techniques, certain patterns appear and reappear, whether made by diligent fingers or copied on mechanical looms.

Makers of *needle lace*, using a short needle almost as fine as a hair, produced designs of infinite complexity. The pattern, usually drawn on parchment that topped two layers of linen base, was used to enable the needlewoman to place the outline threads, which were then connected and embroidered upon by numberless variations of the buttonhole stitch. Some designs were traced with more stitches in a raised-cord outline called a

LACE ACCESSORIES

The revival of interest in needlework that occurred toward the end of the nineteenth century prompted a new line of products. Sara Hadley, a prominent teacher and purveyor of lacemaking supplies, sold thread, tools and patterns from her New York shop. Teneriffe (shown here), and other techniques such as tatting and hairpin lace, employed the fingers and creative instincts of countless women.

cordonnet. Linking separate motifs were meshes or small stitches called brides, or "legs," that soon filled in the background area. When the pattern was completely worked, the supporting backing of parchment and cloth was cut away, leaving the delicate webbing to stand on its own.

Needle lace afforded great latitude in design and in the sizes of pieces to be worked. Freed from the gridwork of a background fabric, the tendrils of lace could twine and twirl as the imagination called, with many lacemaking centers originating their own signature designs. The most popular were then copied and produced in many other lacemaking areas.

Bobbin lace, which developed at roughly the same time as needle lace, could be used for the simplest of edgings or the grandest court wear. Weaving was the basis for bobbin lace, whether of single or multiple threads. A pattern, often of parch-

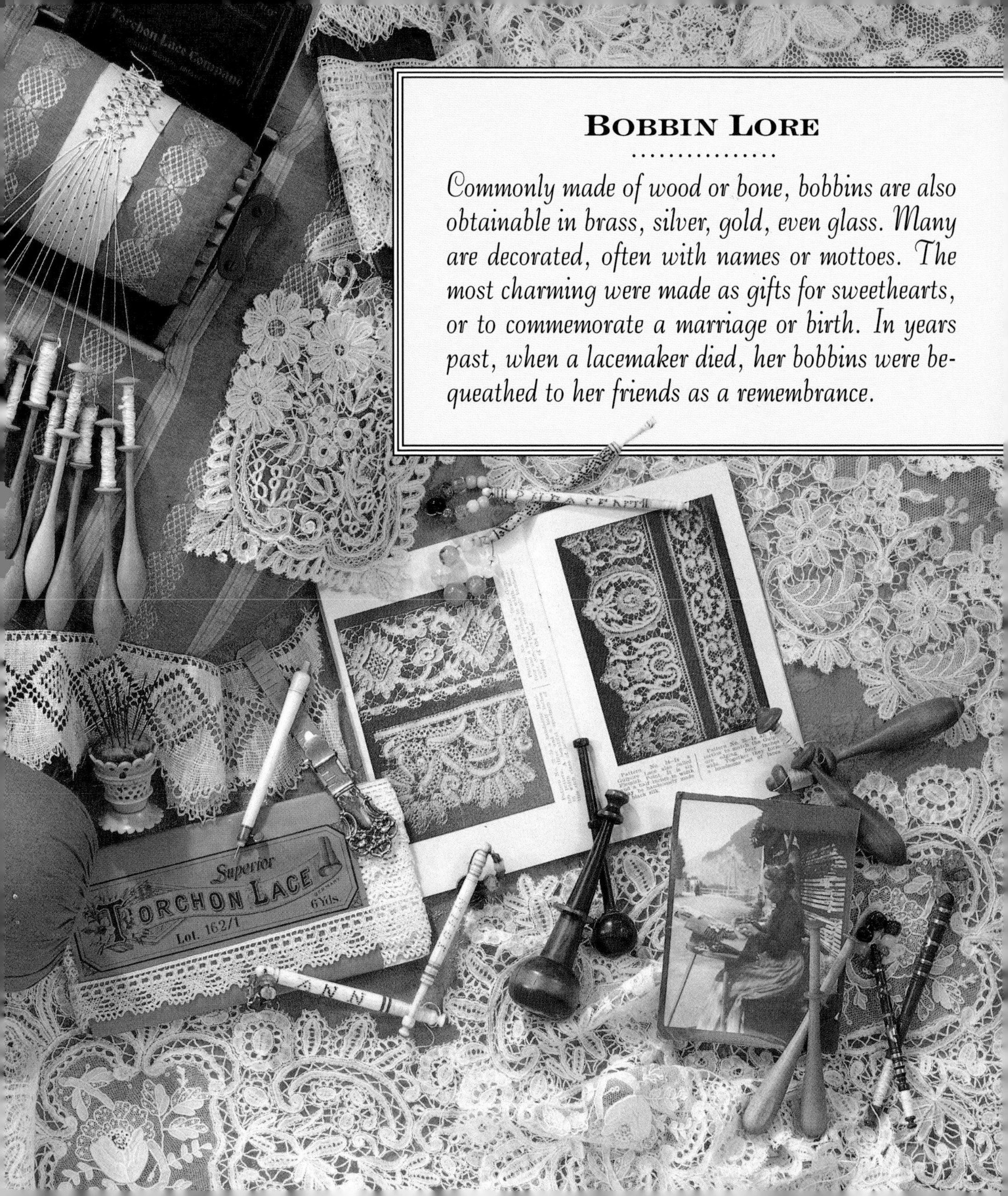

Bobbin Lore

Commonly made of wood or bone, bobbins are also obtainable in brass, silver, gold, even glass. Many are decorated, often with names or mottoes. The most charming were made as gifts for sweethearts, or to commemorate a marriage or birth. In years past, when a lacemaker died, her bobbins were bequeathed to her friends as a remembrance.

ment, was prepared and pinned to a bolster-like pillow that was held in the lap or within a frame. Pins controlled the path of the threads wound on the bobbins, which weighted them. While six dozen bobbins might be prepared for use in a typical design, it was not uncommon to have over a thousand bobbins. Moving across the pillow, the lacemaker would twist and interweave the threads to match the pattern, then flick back across, the bobbins keeping the threads taut.

For even the most experienced makers, the production of each inch of needle lace demanded long hours of labor. Many specialized, producing either the fine mesh of the background or the "motifs" at its center; the elements were then joined together with fine stitchery, allowing pieces much larger than a pillow could afford.

Both bobbin and needle lace are now more likely found in the form of *machine lace.* As early as the eighteenth century, curious and industrious manufacturers of lace were looking for ways to produce more

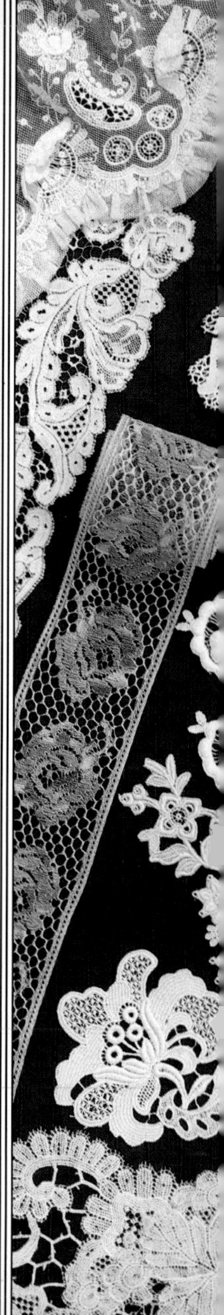

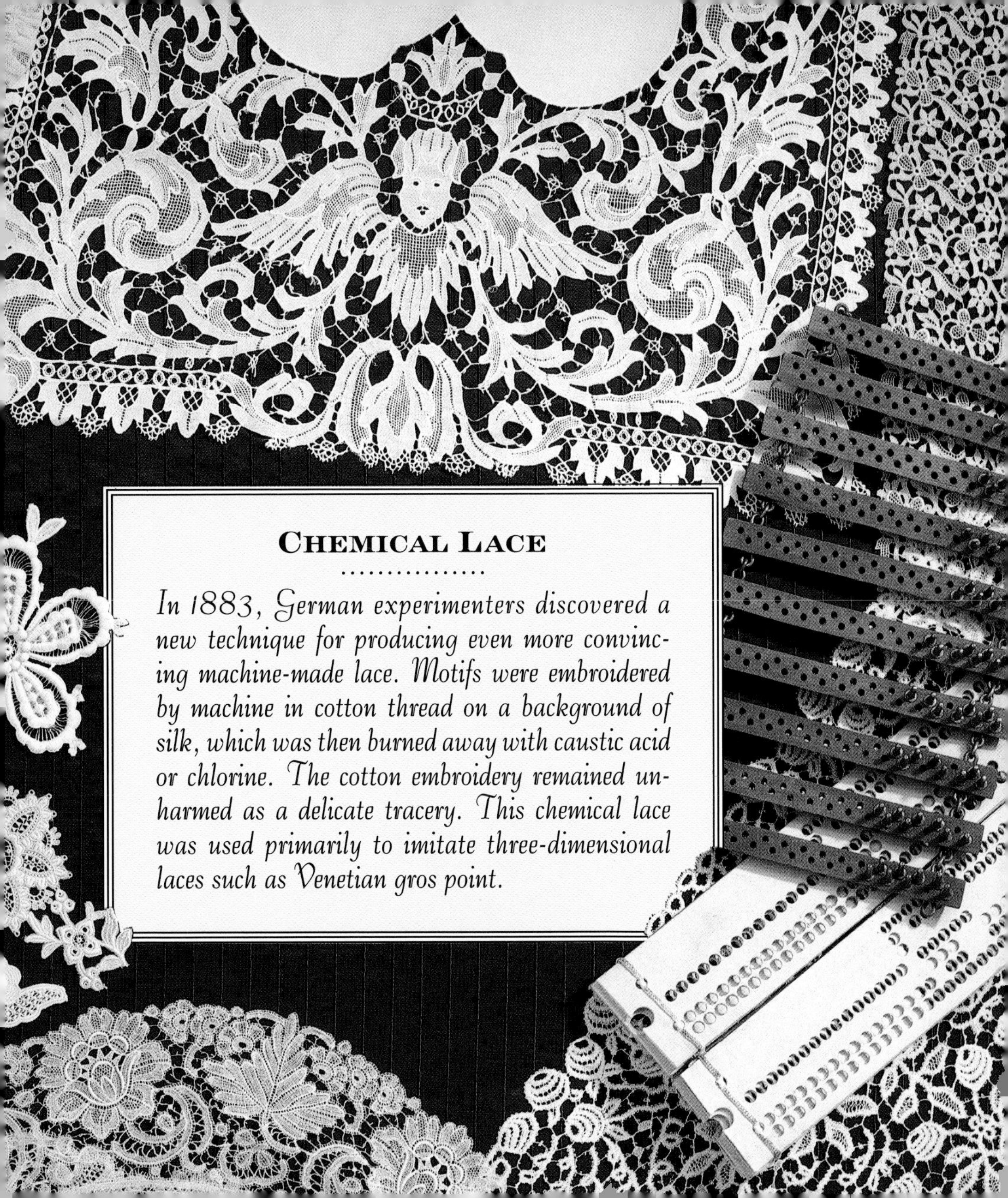

CHEMICAL LACE

In 1883, German experimenters discovered a new technique for producing even more convincing machine-made lace. Motifs were embroidered by machine in cotton thread on a background of silk, which was then burned away with caustic acid or chlorine. The cotton embroidery remained unharmed as a delicate tracery. This chemical lace was used primarily to imitate three-dimensional laces such as Venetian gros point.

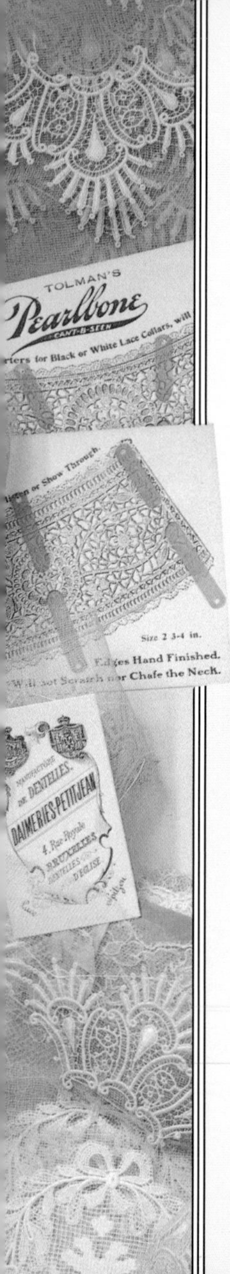

of it at a cheaper price. In 1768, an English stocking manufacturer named Hammond attempted to make lace on his machinery, but produced only a rough net. This led the way to John Leaver's loom, perfected in the early nineteenth century, which could produce long lengths of well-woven web. The machine-made netting was used as the base for hand-embroidered motifs, which could easily be made and sold.

England protected its industrial secrets, but smugglers soon brought knowledge and parts to France. Here, the invention of the Jacquard loom, which wove designs controlled by a system of punched cards, meant that both background and elaborate designs could be produced at the same time. As steam began to power the looms, lace became inexpensive and common, perhaps the prettiest product of the early machine age. Production centered in the French towns of Le Puy-en-Velay and Calais (the latter's name synonymous with machine lace), Nottingham in England and Saint Gall in Switzerland. In time, machine-

BRUXELLES
STRANGERS
ENTRÉE LIBRE
W.J.S.
PARIS NEW-YORK
MADE IN FRANCE
Adresse Télégraphique
LACES
CODE LIEBER
MANUFACTURE DE DENTELLES VÉRITABLES
P. & P. MUYLLE
BRUGES
(Belgique)
EXPORTATION
BRUGES
DUCHESSE
GROS BRUGES
CLUNY
VALENCIENNES
BINCHE
MILAN
POINT DE PARIS
VENISE ETC.
COMPTE CHÈQUES POSTAUX
Nº 133654
16, RUE DES RONCES.
Maison de Détail Grand' place. 14.
P. MOREY,
RIBBONS, LACES, HOSIERY,
At the Cheap Store, 397 Washington St.
LACE FACTORY
GREAT STOCK
of
Ancient Lace
Stylish Damasks
Brocades
for
UPHOLSTERING
Melville & Ziffer
REAL
LACE
BEDCOVERS
CURTAINS
TABLE LINEN
EMBROIDERIES
LACE FANS
VENICE
(OWN LACE FACTORY IN BURANO)
MELVILLE & ZIFFER
MELVILLE & ZIFFER
MELVILLE & ZIFFER — VENISE
Manufacture MELVILLE & ZIFFER
Palais des Doges
ROSALIND
Produced by THE ARNOLD PRINT WORKS.
Chas. A. Stevens & Bros.
111 State St.
Chicago
Special Catalogue
of
SILKS
&
LACES
TWO SAMPLES
OF OUR CELEBRATED
$1.00 SILKS
21 INCHES WIDE
ONLY $1.00 PER YARD.
CHAS. A. STEVENS

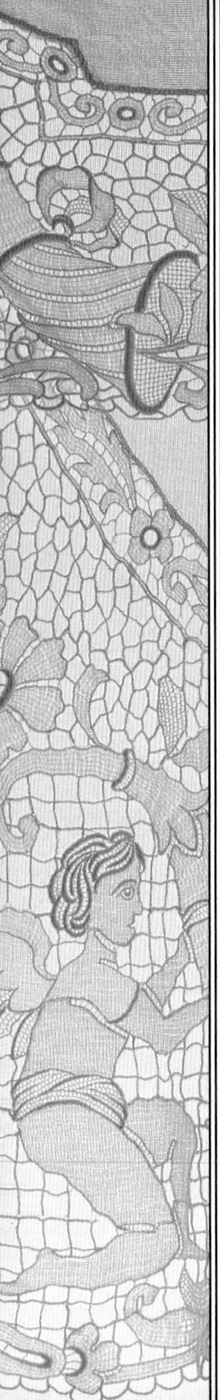

made lace was made a viable substitute for that stitched or woven by patient hands.

Descriptions of each pattern can never replace the personal discovery that each lace brings. Only by touching the line of the design, weighing a scrap in the hand, or marveling at the minute meshes that inform a motif does true appreciation come.

And so a new generation is tied to those who have gone before, by these delicate filaments of fancy, the best of the lacemaker's art. Once men lost fortunes, even their lives, to possess a fine piece of lace; now we merely lose our hearts, for the centuries have yielded us graceful topnotes to our treasure. We love lace for its loveliness, its matchless workmanship, but we respond to something more than its pattern of line and shadow. There is the beauty of translucency, the feminine wile of a fabric that half reveals, half conceals; the innocence of snowy lace that is reserved for festival times, a baby's christening robe or a

bride's veil; the grand luxe of a fabric seemingly as fragile as a cobweb, put to daily use; and, once again, there's the amusement of fashion's dictates.

For those who love lace know that, as in our own lives, there's more to the material than a knot and an arabesque. Only this fabric, substantial as a sigh, bears such a weight of history and romance, all of creation ensnared by a thread.

Below is a categorized list of the types of laces that are shown in this book.

Needlepoint Laces

(created by hand using a single thread and a single needle making a looped buttonhole stitch)

Gros point
Point de Gaze
Point plat de Venise
Gros point nouveau
Needlepoint reseau

Combinations of Handmade Techniques

Lacis (knotted and embroidered)
Macramé (knotted and looped)

Machine-made Laces

Leaver (a twisted thread lace)
Raschel (a warp knit lace)
Machine embroidery on net
Chemical lace (embroidered lace with chemically removed foundation)

Bobbin Laces

(created by hand interlacing multiple threads weighted with bobbins)

Duchesse
Valenciennes
Chantilly
Bobbin guipure
Brussels
Honiton
Torchon

Other Handmade Techniques

Tambour embroidery
Cutwork guipure
Irish crochet
Crochet lace
Deflected and/or withdrawn element lace
Tatting
Teneriffe
Hairpin
Netting
Embroidered lace
Tape lace
Battenberg
Princess applique

Identifications start at the upper center of each two-page spread and continue clockwise.

Cover: Center image; lady in blue, chromolith; 20″ × 15″; c1905; laces, see pp 42—43.
Front Endsheet: Lingerie case; mesh fabric, cloth and rosebud trim; c1920. Handkerchief; silk fabric, machine-made lace, embroidered rosebud trim; c1930. Pair stemmed cloth flowers; c1910. Boxed greeting; celluloid, silk fabric and cord with rosebud trim; c1910. Thread and ribbon wreathes; c1910. Teddy; silk, machine-made lace trim, embroidery; c1930. Ribbon flowers; silk; c1920. Shawl; machine-made lace, silk fabric; c1915. Ribbon flowers; silk; c1990. Ribbon flowers; silk; c1920. Green square; machine embroidery, deflected element frills; c1945. Pink teddy; silk with machine-made lace trim; c1940. Pair painted rectangles; boy/girl, machine-made lace frames; c1915. Bird; chemical lace; c1970.

P. 5. Glove; Irish crochet; c1920. Lace flower; point de Gaze; c1970. Photographer, Marie Spoto.
Pp. 6—7. Fabric; chenille and ribbon appliqué, embroidery; c1920. Capelet; embroidered fabric; c1825. Stock calendar illus.; lady in dressing gown, 20″ × 14.75″, die cut, embossed; c1905. Collar; embroidery, needlepoint lace fills; c1840.
Pp. 8—9. Fabric; machine-made lace, metal-wrapped cord appliqué; c1920. Ballerinas, seated lady; porcelain, Dresden; c1900—1940.
Pp. 10—11. Bedcover; mesh fabric, needlepoint lace; c1930.
Pp. 12—13. Part of panel, Irish crochet; c1890. Border with motto; crochet; c1890. Border with heart motif; crochet; c1900. Hand towel with corner rose medallion; crochet; c1940. Doily; cro-

chet surrounds cutwork cloth center; c1940. Basket, flowers; crochet; c1940. 4 doilies; crochet; c1950. Lace flowers; crochet; c1910.
Pp. 14–15. Border; point de Gaze; c1920.

THE LEGACY OF LACE

Pp. 16–17. Print; *The Chichling Odoriferous of Sicily;* hand-tinted steel engravings from series, A Paris, Publié par François et Louis Janet, London; March 1832; publ. by Ch. Tilt, 86 Fleet St., Imp. Lith de Lemercier. Cuffs; bobbin lace, tape lace elements, needlepoint lace fills; c1910. Print; *The Shamrock of Ireland;* same series. Print; *The Tulip of Holland;* same series.
Pp. 18–19. Tie; square-mesh Valenciennes lace; c1890. Leapfrogging cupids; porcelain; c1880. Metallic lace; tape lace, needlepoint lace reseau; c1910. Narrow border; duchesse lace; c1920. Set of 4 columns, 4 cupid figures; porcelain, Dresden; c1880. Lace panels; Brussels bobbin lace, c1900.
Pp. 20–21. Needle case; carved vegetable ivory; c1885. Pomander; egg shape; carved, drilled vegetable ivory; c1885. Caul (bonnet back); needlepoint lace (point plat de Venise); 17th c. Pincushion; c1890. Pair buttons; faux amethyst and rhinestone, c1890. Heart-shape ring; gold, garnet; c1900. Border; needlepoint lace; c1890. Scrap; bejeweled lady; die cut, embossed; c1880. Border; tape lace; c1890.
Pp. 22–23. 2 lengths of insert; knotted mesh fabric, embroidered; c1930. 2 butterflies, small square; knotted mesh, embroidered; c1910. Rectangle with heart; crochet; c1920. Textile with ribbon edge; 16th c. Knotted fabric, knotted round; c1890. Netting shuttles; metal; c1900. Netting shuttle; bone; c1900. Lacis in working frame; c1890. Chatelaine; c1880. Metallic floral sprig; embroidery, cord; c1900. Unicorn panel; lacis; 16th c. Knotted fabrics; c1910.
Pp. 24–25. 2 large motif laces; gros point nouveau; c1880. Border; needlepoint lace with appliqué tape; c1900. Needlepoint lace; c1890. Fleur-de-lis pin, c1910. Lace panel gros point nouveau, needlepoint lace edging; c1880. Border; needlepoint lace; c1890. Lace square; needlepoint lace; c1930. Ring with blue faux gems; c1930. Ring with green faux gems; c1940. Lace; gros point; 17th c. Pendant with faux emerald; c1925. Ring, faux rubies and diamonds; c1940. Tablecloth remnant, needlepoint lace, c1880.
Pp. 26–27. Flounce; point de Gaze; c1880. Jacquard ribbon trim; golden birds on red ground; c1890. Sewing bird; brass; c1860. Edging; metallic machine-made lace; c1930. Border; machine-made lace; c1890.
Pp. 28–29. Tie; Princess appliqué lace; c1900. Tie; duchesse lace, point de Gaze medallions; c1890. Hand, magnifying glass; c1940. Chromolith print, 2 women in lace, 11.25″×8″; c1895. Cat; porcelain, jointed; c1880. Doll; bisque, with duchesse lace fichu, machine-made skirt dress trim; c1900. Pocket watch; gold; c1880. Doll; 10″ Kestner "Gibson Girl"; c1900: doll clothes; machine-embroidered dress, machine-made lace collar; c1980. Wreath; embroidered appliqué; c1910. Doll; French bisque with wardrobe of machine-made lace trim; papier-mâché fabric-covered egg; c1890. Necklace; seed pearls, gold; c1900. Tasseled pillow; crochet lace cover; c1950. Pins; freshwater pearls, gold; c1910. Box; machine-made lace, scrap figure; c1890. Beads, seed pearls; c1920. Veil; appliqué tape lace; c1910.
Pp. 30–31. Bertha; point de Gaze; c1880. Fan; hand-painted paper, faux spangles; c1860. Handkerchief; point de Gaze border; c1880. Fan; hand-painted, polychrome bone; 18th c. Teardrop medallions; point de Gaze; c1920. Rug border; jacquard wool; c1880. Fan cover; point de Gaze; c1880.
Pp. 32–33. Mantilla; Chantilly lace; c1860. Fan; hand-painted silk with spangles and ribbon trim; c1890. Woven fabric adaptation of Pierre Cot's *The Storm;* painted 1880. Brooch; "gutta percha"; c1870.
Pp. 34–35. Square; embroidery, needlepoint lace medallions and border; c1910. Valentine; coffeepot with paper honeycomb and applied scrap, die cut, embossed; c1900. Cuff; embroidered; c1910. Calendar; colonial man and woman; c1901. Gloves; crochet; c1930. Border; machine-embroidered mesh fabric; c1910. Theater cards; c1880. Calendar; colonial man and woman, foldout; c1897. Rectangle; machine-embroidered mesh fabric; c1905. Card; chromolith print; 3 girls in costume; c1890.
Pp. 36–37. 6 prints; women in lace garments, hand-tinted steel engravings with paper lace

borders; le voile; le fichu; le bague; le schall; la couronne; la mantille; c1850. Sprigged textile; machine-made mesh fabric trim; c1910.

Pp. 38–39. Lace fabric; cutwork guipure lace with needlepoint lace fills; c1900. Collar; cutwork guipure lace with tape elements, embroidery; c1910. Porcelain dove; c1880. Boy, dog; painted porcelain; c1885.

Pp. 40–41. Front and back dress panels; pineapple fiber piña cloth, embroidered, with applied silk ribbon flowers, machine-made lace insert; c1920.

Pp. 42–43. Bodice; mesh fabric overlay, tambour embroidery, ribbon appliqué; c1895. Butterflies; 2 bobbin lace, 7 needlepoint lace; c1900. Lace flower; point de Gaze; c1970. Belt buckle, carved ivory; c1900. Chromolith seed company advertising poster, lady with flowers and fairies; J. Ottman, N.Y., 31″ × 22″; c1896.

THE LANGUAGE OF LACE

Pp. 44–45. Dress; Chemical lace collar/sleeve trim; c1905. Floral spray; ribbons; c1991. Print; boy smelling rose; c1900. Valentine; 2 girls amid pansies, die cut, embossed; c1900. Handkerchief case; embroidery bobbin lace border; c1940. Stock calendar; 2 girls in boat, imprinted Henry Hoeltzel Lancaster, Pa., die cut, embossed, 17″ × 10.25″; c1905.

Pp. 46–47. Medallion; Battenberg lace and appliqué; c1910. Petticoat; machine-made lace, embroidery; c1895. Bag with pendant balls; crochet; c1900. Chromolith print, girl with rose garland, 17″ × 13″; c1890.

Pp. 48–49. Dressing coat; embroidery, with medallion and tassel of interlaced, knotted cord; c1895. Lingerie case; multicolor embroidery; c1920. Handkerchief; chemical lace border; c1950. Handkerchief; patchwork of machine-made lace, embroidered inserts; c1920. Handkerchief; tape lace border; c1920. Handkerchief; Battenberg lace border; c1920. Handkerchief; Honiton lace border; c1890.

Pp. 50–51. Bead decoration; c1895. Chromolith prints; "Gay Nineties" ladies; c1890. "Pearl" sprig; c1960. Jeweled belt buckle; c1910. Buttons; brass, faux jewels; c1890. Bodice; Paris; c1890. Lace over bodice; bobbin appliqué lace; c1890.

Pp. 52–53. Flounce; machine-made lace; c1910. Child, carriage; porcelain; c1920. Woman, cupid in shell; painted bisque; c1880.

Pp. 54–55. Rose printed textile; c1910. Chromolith illus.; children, roses, die cut, embossed, 17″ × 11.5″; c1895. Cuff; chemical lace, needlepoint lace edge pyramids; c1920. Scrap; child, flowers; die cut, embossed; c1885. Bow, pendant balls; silk; c1900.

Pp. 56–57. Panel; embroidered mesh fabric, needlepoint lace fills; c1880. Chromolith prints; ladies in lace; die cut, embossed; c1890. Parasol with thread tassels; shadow-stitch embroidery, machine-made lace trim; c1890. Parasol with chenille tassels; c1890.

Pp. 58–59. Wax flower bridal headpiece; c1915. Jell-O advertising brochure; bride, flower girl; c1918. Scrap; brides; die cut, embossed; c1890. Scrap; doves; die cut, embossed; c1890. Flower; Irish crochet; c1910. Chromolith print; *An Easter Bride;* 28″ × 20″; c1890. Ribbon frame; embroidered, silk; c1930. Bridal tiara; wax flowers with rhinestone heart; c1910. Bride and groom dolls; 4″ porcelain; c1910. Corsage; wax flowers, fabric leaves; c1890. Frog; knotted, interlaced cords; c1900. Salesman's sample; bridal dress; Irish crochet collar and inserts, crochet lace edgings; c1890. Scraps; die cut, embossed, c1880. Bridal headpiece; wax flowers, fabric leaves and rosebuds; c1890. Paper nosegay; multilayer foldout; die cut, embossed with applied machine-made lace; c1920.

Pp. 60–61. Ecru bonnet; tatting, ribbon trim; c1900. White bonnet; knitting, crochet and blue ribbon trim; c1930. Uncut scrap sheet; crying, laughing babies; c1900. Trade card; baby blue seat; trimmed; c1880. Scrap; baby in red chair; die cut, embossed; c1885. Bonnet; embroidered mesh fabric, lace and ribbon trim; c1900. Trade card; girl in top hat; trimmed; c1890. Scrap; baby in bassinet; die cut, embossed; c1880. Quilted coverlet; c1890. Scraps; child with rabbit, baby with rattle, child with doll, die cut, embossed; c1885. Doll; machine-made lace trim on dress and pantaloons; c1880. Baby shoes; white fabric, embroidered; c1940. Scrap; woman and child; die cut, embossed; c1885. Pink bonnet; embroidered and lace-trimmed edges, ribbon; c1930. White bonnet; embroidered cloth; machine-made lace trim; c1910.

Pp. 62–63. *Harper's Bazaar;* June 17, 1893. Border; black machine-made lace; late 19th–20th c. Fashion page; c1890. Neckpiece with fall; machine-made lace inserts; c1890. Photo; woman in bridal costume; c1880. Neckpiece; tape lace; c1890. Fashion page, *Harper's Bazaar;* c1890. *Harper's Bazaar;* July 15, 1893. Photo of boy in lace collar; c1890. Black lace; machine-made; c1900. Beaded ornament; c1880. Fashion page; c1890. Fashion page; c1875. Fashion page; *Harper's Bazaar;* Jan. 25, 1873.
Pp. 64–65. Silk ribbon roses; c1920. Bodice; machine-made lace; c1900. Jabot; white lace; machine-made; c1910. Silk ribbon rose garland; c1918. Lingerie, embroidered mesh fabric; c1920. Lingerie; machine-made lace border; c1918.

THE MANY FACES OF LACE

Pp. 66–67. Tablecloth, napkins; alternating squares, cloth and embroidered mesh fabric; c1920. Heart-shape medallion, round medallion, tea set; all jasperware; c1890.
Pp. 68–69. Tablecloth; tableau, embroidered knotted mesh, needlepoint lace medallion, bobbin lace surrounds, cutwork swags; c1910.
Pp. 70–71. Curtain; machine-made lace, applied braid edging; c1920. Book; *Ancestry and Future of the Modern Lace Curtain* by W.M. Laurel Harris given away by The Quaker Lace Co. in 1919. Forbes & Wallace advertising brochure card; c1905. Receipt; M. Jesurum & Cie, Venice; 1910. Vase-shaped ornament; appliqué and embroidery; Chinese; c1920. Lace square; needlepoint lace, Hungarian style; c1920. Silk cocoons. Printed textile; toile; c1850.
Pp. 72–73. Yoke and border; Irish crochet; c1905. Large butterfly; knotted mesh, embroidered; c1900. Small butterflies; point de Gaze; c1900. Chromolith print; lady in blue, 20″ × 15″; c1905. Chair; porcelain; c1910. Small doll; porcelain; c1900. Larger doll; duchesse lace fichu, machine-made skirt dress trim; bisque, c.1900. Tiny paper doll, die cut; c1880. Chromolith print, dress-up wedding; c1880.
Pp. 74–75. Hat veil; tambour embroidery, embroidered mesh fills; c1840. Fashion plate; hand-colored engravings; c1809. Fashion plate; hand-colored engravings; c1809. Christening dress or child's undergarment; withdrawn element, deflected element, openwork embroidery; c1830. Table runner; embroidery, mesh grounds are deflected element work; c1870.
Pp. 76–77. Tablecloth; finished as cutwork guipure lace; c1925. Antimacassar, with Esus Osser—God of the Forest; needlepoint lace; c1900. Chatelaine; scissor with case, writing tablet with pencil, pincushion, thimble holder, thimble; sterling silver; c1879.
Pp. 78–79. Butterfly, floral medallions, tassels; Irish crochet; c1890. Scissors; c1880. Crochet hook and case; c1920. Thread; Barbour's; c1910. Collar; Irish crochet; c1910. Medallions; crochet; c1910.
Pp. 80–81. 4 panels; tape lace, needlepoint lace animals; French; c1925.
Pp. 82–83. Cuff; point de Gaze; c1870.

THE FINE ART OF LACE

Pp. 84–85. Fabric; chenille embroidery, ribbon applique; c1890. Pricking, pins, bobbins, medallion; bobbin lace; 20th c. Blueprint of bobbin lace; 20th c. Pouncer; c1880. 3 eyelet stilettos; c1880. Man's wedding handkerchief; withdrawn element embroidery; c1880. Needlepoint lace in progress; c1970. 2 strawberries; needle/pin cleaners; c1890. Sampler; needlepoint lace stitches; c1920. Sample book; crochet, tape lace flower; c1920. Workbook; design sketches; c1825–40. Book of lace designs; Henri Lemaire; c1880. Handkerchief; bobbin lace border; c1950. Handkerchief; copy of above by Elsie Straight; c1950.
Pp. 86–87. Instruction sheet; tape lace illustrated; c1870. Runner; tape lace; c1900. Neckpiece; black Battenberg lace; c1885. Tape lace in progress; c1905. Instruction sheet; *Harper's Bazaar,* tape lace illustration; c1870. Butterfly; tape lace; c1920. Roll of machine-made tape for making tape lace; c1890. Lacemaking manual; *The Art of Modern Lace Making:* tape lace illustrated; publ. 1891. Apron; Battenburg lace trim; c1915.
Pp. 88–89. Fringe; macramé; c1885. Instruction manual; *Treasure of Use and Beauty,* publ. 1883. Illus., macramé lace; *Le Macrame,* publ. 1912. Border; metallic and beads; tape and needlepoint lace; c1890. Illus., macramé lace principle knots; *Le Macramé,* publ. 1912. Instruction

manual; macramé illustrated; *Le Macramé*, publ. 1912.

Pp. 90–91. Laces; tatting; 20th c. Tatting shuttle; tortoise; c1890. Tatting shuttle; sterling; c1890. Thread carrier; bone; c1890. Teneriffe loom with pins; c1900. Black teneriffe loom, envelope; Proctor; c1890. Teneriffe laces; c1910. Teneriffe pillow; "Sara Hadley's Teneriffe Cushion"; c1900. Sara Hadley ad 1891. Heart pin-keeper; c1890. Manual; S.H. Lilla Hailstone, *Designs for Lace Making;* c1885. Larger hairpin lace loom; 20th c. Small hairpin lace loom; c1890. Handkerchief; tatted lace border; c1930. Stiletto; c1895. Runner; hairpin lace; c1910.

Pp. 92–93. Teardrop medallion; duchesse lace; 1st half 20th c. Lacemaking manual; *Practical Lace Making,* Torchon Lace Co., St. Louis (for Princess Lace Pillow); c1915. Bobbin lacemaking pillow; with Belgian style bobbins; c1915. Border; torchon lace; c1900. Border; duchesse lace; c1920. Collar bobbin lace motifs, needlepoint lace ground; c1900. Flounce; appliqué bobbin lace, duchesse lace border; c1910. Rectangle; duchesse lace; c1920. Lacemaking manual; *Practical Lace Making* (as above). Pair bobbins; sold with Princess Loom lacemaking pillow; Torchon Lace Co., St. Louis; c1915. 2 wood/metal bobbins (not a pair); English "Midlands" style; c1890. Pair wood bobbins; c1900. Photo, lacemaker; Belgian-style pillow; c1885. Collar; duchesse lace; c1910. Smaller bulbous end bobbin; Spanish (?); 19th–20th c. Larger bulbous end bobbin; used with large bolster pillow; 19th–20th c. 2 bone bobbins; English "Midlands" style; inscribed ". . . by one I love," "John Nail Pheasant"; c1850. Border in "Torchon Lace" wrapper; machine-made lace; c1890. Pricker (to make holes in bobbin lace patterns); 19th–early 20th c. Gauge; sterling; c1880. Pincushion; vegetable ivory; c1885. Lacemaking pillow; torchon lace; c1930. 12 pair beaded Scandinavian-style bobbins; 19th–early 20th c. Border; "Russian peasant" bobbin lace; late 19th–early 20th c. Border; duchesse lace; c1920. 2 bobbins; English "Midlands" style; inscribed "Ann," "John"; c1870. Large teardrop shape; bobbin guipure lace; c1900. Border with bird; bobbin lace, virgin ground; c1910. Border with dog; bobbin lace, point de Paris ground; c1890. Pricking; bobbin lace pattern; Dutch; c1840.

Pp. 94–95. Ruffle-edge border; machine-embroidered mesh fabric; c1890. Runner; chemical lace; c1890. Border; chemical lace; 20th c. Jacquard pattern cards and wooden bars for lace machines; 19th c. Flounce; chemical lace; c1900. Collar; chemical lace; c1890. Collar; chemical lace; c1910. 2 floral medallions; chemical lace; 20th c. Medallion, embroidery, needlepoint lace fills; c1890. Polychrome insert; machine-made lace; c1925. Flounce; machine-made lace; c1900. 2 borders; chemical laces; c1910.

Pp. 96–97. Border; embroidered mesh fabric; "Made in Germany"; c1910. Business card; Bertha Buge, Royal Lace Manufactory; c1900. Business card; T. Stappers, Antwerp, Belgium; c1890. Business card; The Lace Store, Havana, Cuba; c1920. Border; machine-made lace, embroidered; "W.J.S., Paris New York, Made in France"; c1910. Bodice; chemical lace; c1895. Business card; P&P Muylle; Bruges; c1880. Business card; P. Morey; c1890. Business card; Melville & Ziffer; with photo of lacemakers; c1890. Notepad; Melville & Ziffer; Venice; c1890. Printed plate; lace design with birds; Graham; c1842. Fashion plate; advertisement for Sweetsen Penbrook & Co, "Rosalind"—model shown in Place de la Concorde, Paris; c1900. Catalog with dressing tables; Manifattura Merletti, Milan; c1908. Catalog; Chas A. Stevens & Bros.; 1891. Sample card, swatches; Chas A. Stevens & Bros; 1891. Catalog; tape lace handkerchief patterns; C.S. Davidsson, N.Y.; c1904. Business card; G.V.S. Quackenbush; c1880. Paper card; lace print on blue ground; c1850. Receipt; Voss & Stern; 1889. Business card; Societe Dentelliere Gruyerienne; c1916. Business card; Odile Matthys; c1890. Border; chemical lace; c1900. Medallions; chemical lace; c1910. Business card; Daimeries-Pettijean; c1880. Cards with collar supports; c1890.

Pp. 98–99. Curtains, valance; machine-made lace; c1940. Insert photo; lacemaker's lamp, glass; c1870; edging; bobbin lace; c1920; cuff; needlepoint lace; c1890.

Back Endsheet: Same as front endsheet except for addition of sachet bag; ribbon and machine-made lace trim; c1910.